Nick Vandome

Photoshop Elements 14
Tips, Tricks & Shortcuts

For Windows and Mac

In easy steps is an imprint of In Easy Steps Limited
16 Hamilton Terrace · Holly Walk · Leamington Spa
Warwickshire · United Kingdom · CV32 4LY
www.ineasysteps.com

Notice of Liability
Every effort has been made to ensure that this book contains accurate
and current information. However, In Easy Steps Limited and the
author shall not be liable for any loss or damage suffered by readers
as a result of any information contained herein.

Trademarks
Photoshop® is a registered trademark of Adobe Systems Incorporated.
All other trademarks are acknowledged as belonging to their
respective companies.

In Easy Steps Limited supports The Forest Stewardship Council (FSC),
the leading international forest certification organization. All our titles
that are printed on Greenpeace approved FSC certified paper carry the
FSC logo.

MIX
Paper from
responsible sources
FSC® C020837
FSC
www.fsc.org

Printed and bound in the United Kingdom

ISBN 978-1-84078-716-0

Contents

1 Introducing Elements

Photoshop Elements
is a digital image
editing program that
comprehensively spans the
gap between very basic
programs and professional-
level ones. This chapter
introduces the various
workspaces and modes of
Elements, shows how to
access them, and details what
can be done with each one.

Photoshop Elements can be bought online directly from Adobe, as well as from other computer and software sites, or at computer software stores. There are Windows and Mac versions of the program, and with Elements 14 these are virtually identical. If Elements 14 is bought from the Adobe website, at **www.adobe.com**, it can be downloaded and installed directly from there. Otherwise it will be provided on a DVD, with a serial number that needs to be entered during installation.

The New icon pictured above indicates a new or enhanced feature introduced with the latest version of Photoshop Elements 14.

About Elements

Photoshop Elements is the offspring of the professional-level image-editing program, Photoshop. Photoshop is somewhat unusual in the world of computer software, in that it is widely accepted as being the best program of its type on the market. If professional designers or photographers are using an image-editing program, it will almost certainly be Photoshop. However, two of the potential drawbacks to Photoshop are its cost and its complexity. This is where Elements comes into its own. Adobe (the maker of Photoshop and Elements) has recognized that the majority of digital imaging users (i.e. the consumer market) want something with the basic power of Photoshop, but with enough user-friendly features to make it easy to use. With the explosion in the digital camera market, a product was needed to meet the needs of a new generation of image editors – and that product is Photoshop Elements.

Elements contains most of the same powerful editing/color management tools as the full version of Photoshop, and it also includes a number of versatile features for sharing images and for creating artistic projects, such as slideshows, cards, calendars and cover photos for Facebook. It also has valuable features, such as the Guided edit and Quick edit modes, where you can quickly apply editing techniques and follow step-by-step processes to achieve a range of creative and artistic effects.

Special effects

One of the great things about using Elements with digital images is that it provides numerous fun and creative options for turning mediocre images into eye-catching works of art. This is achieved

through a wide variety of guided activities within Guided edit mode, which have been added to and enhanced in Elements 14.

Advanced features

In addition to user-friendly features, Elements also has an Expert editing mode where you can use a range of advanced features, including a full set of tools for editing and color adjustments.

Welcome Screen

When you first open Elements, you will be presented with the Welcome Screen. This offers initial advice about working with Elements and also provides options for accessing the different workspaces. The Welcome Screen appears by default, but this can be altered once you become more familiar with Elements.

Welcome Screen functions

1 Options for organizing photos, editing them and using them in a variety of creative ways

2 Click on the **Organizer** button to go to that area

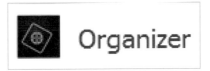

3 Click on the **Photo Editor** button to go to that area

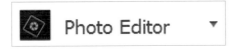

Hot tip

The Welcome Screen can be accessed at any time by selecting **Help > Welcome Screen** from the Photo Editor or Organizer Menu bar. Click on this button at the top of the Welcome Screen to select options for what happens when Elements is launched.

Don't forget

The **Video Editor** button on the Welcome Screen links to Adobe Premiere Elements (sold separately) which is the video editing companion app to Photoshop Elements.

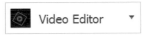

Don't forget

In Elements 14 there is also an **eLive** button on the top toolbar. This links to a range of help and news articles about Elements.

Don't forget

The Elements Organizer can be accessed from any of the Editor modes by clicking on the Organizer button on the Taskbar.

Hot tip

The keyboard shortcut for closing Elements is Ctrl + Q (Command key + Q on a Mac).

Photo Editor Workspace

From the Welcome Screen, the Photo Editor workspace can be accessed. This is a combination of the work area (where images are opened and edited), menus, toolbars, toolboxes and panels. At first it can seem a little daunting, but Elements has been designed with three different editing modes to give you as many options as possible for editing your photos.

The components of the Photo Editor (Editor) are:

Menu bar   Editor mode buttons   Panels bin

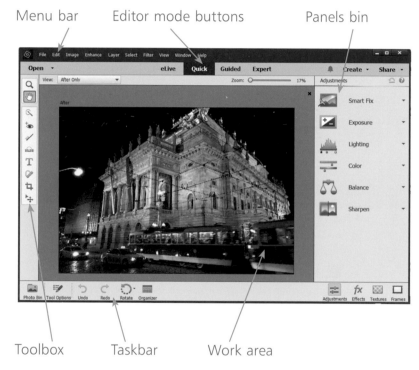

Toolbox   Taskbar   Work area

Editor modes

The three different modes in the Photo Editor are accessed from the buttons at the top of the Elements window. They are:

- **Quick edit mode**. This can be used to perform quick editing options in one step.

- **Guided edit mode**. This can be used to perform a range of editing techniques in a step-by-step process for each.

- **Expert edit mode**. This can be used for the ultimate control over the editing process.

...cont'd

Taskbar and Tool Options

The Taskbar is the group of buttons that is available across all three Editor modes, at the bottom left of the Elements window:

One of the options on the Taskbar is Tool Options. This displays the available options for any tool selected from the Toolbox (different tools are available in each of the different Editor modes). See pages 18-19 for details.

Photo Bin

The Photo Bin is another feature that can be accessed from all three Editor modes. The Photo Bin enables you to quickly access all of the images that you have open within the Editor. To use the Photo Bin:

1 Open two or more images. The most recently-opened one will be the one that is active in the Editor window

2 All open images are shown here in the Photo Bin

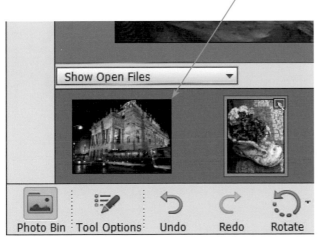

3 Click on an image in the Photo Bin to make that the active one for editing

Don't forget

The items on the Taskbar are, from left to right, show or hide the Photo Bin, show or hide the Tool Options bar, Undo the previous actions, Redo any undone actions, Rotate the active photo, and access the Organizer. In Expert mode there is also an option to change the Layout.

11

Hot tip

Images can also be made active for editing by dragging them directly from the Photo Bin and dropping them within the Editor window.

Hot tip

When an image has started to be edited, this icon appears at its top right-hand corner in the Photo Bin.

Quick Edit Mode

Quick edit mode contains a number of functions that can be selected from panels and applied to an image, without the need to manually apply all of the commands. To do this:

Don't forget

For a more detailed look at Quick edit mode, see pages 80-85.

Don't forget

Some of the options in the Adjustments panel in Quick edit mode (Step 3) have an **Auto** option for applying the effect in a single click.

Don't forget

Move the cursor over one of the thumbnails to view a real-time preview of the effect on the open image. Click on one of the thumbnails to apply the effect.

1 In the Editor, click on the **Quick** button

2 The currently-active image is displayed within the Quick edit window. This has the standard Taskbar and Photo Bin, and a reduced Toolbox. Click here to access the Quick edit panels

3 Select one of the commands to have it applied to the active image. This can be applied either by clicking on one of the thumbnail options or by dragging the appropriate slider at the top of the panel

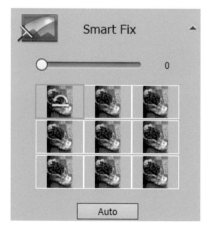

4 Click on these buttons at the bottom of the Quick edit panel to select **Adjustments**, **Effects**, **Textures** and **Frames** options for adding to photos

Guided Edit Mode

Guided edit mode focuses on common tasks for editing digital images, and shows you how to perform them with a step-by-step process. To use Guided edit mode:

1 In the Editor, click on the **Guided** button

2 The Guided edit window contains a range of categories that can be accessed from buttons at the top of the window. Each category contains Guided edit options. Drag the mouse over each item to view the before and after effect

3 Each item has its own wizard to perform the required task. This will take you through a step-by-step process for undertaking the selected action. Move through the steps to complete the selected Guided edit option

Guided edit mode is a great place to start if you are new to image editing, or feel unsure about anything to do with it.

There are new effects added to the Guided edits in Elements 14.

Different Guided edits have varying numbers of steps in the required wizards, but the process is similar for all of them.

13

Expert Edit Mode

Expert edit mode is where you can take full editing control over your photos. It has a range of powerful editing tools so that you can produce subtle and impressive effects. To use Expert mode:

1 In the Editor, click on the **Expert** button

2 The full range of editing tools is available

Expert mode Toolbox   Open panels

14

Taskbar Layout button   Expert mode Panel buttons

The **Layout** button is the one addition on the Taskbar within Expert mode, as opposed to Quick and Guided edit modes. Click on the **Layout** button to access options for the display of your open photos within the Editor window.

Column and Rows
Rows and Column
All Grid
All Column
All Row
All Floating
Default

Layout   Organizer

...cont'd

The Expert Toolbox

The Toolbox in Expert mode contains tools for applying a wide range of editing techniques. Some of the tools have more than one option. To see if a tool has additional options:

1 Move the cursor over the **Toolbox**. Tools that have additional options appear with a small arrow in the top right-hand corner of their icons. Click on a tool to view the options within the Tool Options panel

The tools that have additional options are: Marquee, Lasso, Quick Selection, Healing Brush, Type, Smart Brush, Eraser, Brush, Stamp, Shape, Blur and Sponge.

The default Toolbox tools are (keyboard shortcut in brackets):

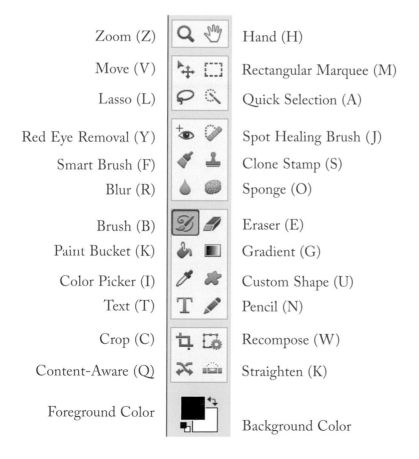

Zoom (Z)	Hand (H)
Move (V)	Rectangular Marquee (M)
Lasso (L)	Quick Selection (A)
Red Eye Removal (Y)	Spot Healing Brush (J)
Smart Brush (F)	Clone Stamp (S)
Blur (R)	Sponge (O)
Brush (B)	Eraser (E)
Paint Bucket (K)	Gradient (G)
Color Picker (I)	Custom Shape (U)
Text (T)	Pencil (N)
Crop (C)	Recompose (W)
Content-Aware (Q)	Straighten (K)
Foreground Color	Background Color

Keyboard shortcuts can be used by pressing the Shift key and the appropriate letter.

Hold down the Alt key and click on the tools in the Toolbox to scroll through the additional options, if available.

15

The panels are located in the Panel Bin, which is at the right of the Editor window. In Expert edit mode this can be collapsed or expanded by selecting **Window > Panel Bin** from the Menu bar.

Some panels can be opened directly with keyboard shortcuts. These are: Effects F6; Graphics F7; Info F8; Histogram F9; History F10; Layers F11 and Navigator F12.

Select **Window > Reset Panels** from the Menu bar to revert the panels to their original format. This is useful if you have been working with several panels and want to revert to the default.

...cont'd

Panels

In Expert edit mode, Elements uses panels to group together similar editing functions and provide quick access to certain techniques. The available panels are:

- **Actions**. This can be used to perform automated actions over a group of images at the same time.

- **Adjustments**. This can be used to add or make editing changes to adjustment layers in the Layers panel.

- **Color Swatches**. This is a panel for selecting colors that can then be applied to parts of an image, or elements that have been added to it.

- **Effects**. This contains special effects and styles that can be applied to an entire image or a selected part of an image. There are also filters which have their own dialog boxes, in which settings can be applied and adjusted. Layer Styles can also be applied to elements within an image.

- **Favorites**. This is where favorite graphical elements from the Content panel can be stored and retrieved quickly.

- **Graphics**. This contains graphical elements that can be added to images, including backgrounds, frame shapes and text.

- **Histogram**. This displays a graph of the tonal range of the colors in an image. It is useful for assessing the overall exposure of an image, and it changes as an image is edited.

- **History**. This can be used to undo any editing steps that have been performed. Every action is displayed and can be reversed by dragging the slider next to the most recent item.

- **Info**. This displays information about an image, or a selected element within it. This includes details about the color in an image or the position of a certain item.

- **Layers**. This enables several layers to be included within an image. This can be useful if you want to add elements to an existing image, such as shapes or text.

- **Navigator**. This can be used to move around an image and magnify certain areas of it.

Working with panels

The default Expert edit mode panels (Layers, Effects, Graphics and Favorites) are located at the right-hand side of the Taskbar. Additional panels can also be accessed from here. To work with panels in Expert edit mode:

1 Click on one of the panel buttons on the Taskbar to open the related panel

2 If there are additional tabs for a panel, click on the tab to view the other options

Click here to access the menu for an open panel.

3 Click on the **More** button to view the rest of the available panels

Actions
Adjustments
Color Swatches
Histogram
History
Info
Navigator

Custom Workspace

More

Do not have too many panels open at one time. If you do, the screen will become cluttered and it will be difficult to edit images effectively.

4 The additional panels are grouped together. Click on a tab to access the required panel. Click and drag on a tab to move the panel away from the rest of the group

Tool Options Bar

When a tool is selected from the Toolbox, in either Expert or Quick mode, the Tool Options bar is activated on the Taskbar. This provides options for selecting different tools from that category (if there are any), and also settings for the currently selected tool. To use the Tool Options bar:

Don't forget

Use these buttons in the top right-hand corner of the Tool Options bar to, from left to right: access the Help options for the selected tool; access the Tool Options menu; or hide the Tool Options bar (click on a tool to display the Tool Options bar again).

1 Select a tool from the Toolbox

2 Click here on the Taskbar to hide or show the Tool Options bar

3 The Tool Options bar is positioned above the Taskbar at the bottom of the Elements window

4 Click here to select different tools from the selected category (in this example it is the Brush tool, the Impressionist Brush tool or the Color Replacement tool)

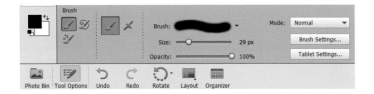

Hot tip

Brush **Mode** has several options for how the brush stroke interacts with the background behind it, e.g. Color Burn, Lighten or Soft Light. These can be used to create artistic effects with the Brush tool and the photo itself.

5 For each item there are different settings available, e.g. for the Brush tool there is **Brush** type, **Size** and **Opacity** (how much of the background is visible through the selected brush stroke). There are also options for a wider range of Brush **Mode** and **Brush Settings**

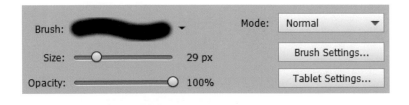

6 Other tools have different settings available from the Tool Options bar. For instance, the **Zoom** tool has options for zooming the currently active image to different magnifications, and also viewing it at specific sizes, e.g. **1:1**, **Fit Screen**, **Fill Screen** and **Print Size**

For a more detailed look at Brush style settings, see pages 156-157.

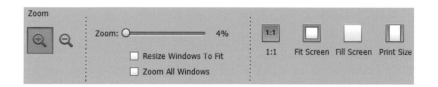

7 The **Text** tools have options for font type, font style, font color, font size, leading (the space between lines of text), bold, italics, underline, strikethrough and also text alignment (left, center or right)

The Text tools also have options for changing the orientation of text and also Text Warp for special effects, see page 148 for details.

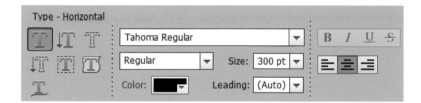

8 For the **Marquee** tools and the **Lasso** tools there are options for editing a current selection (add to selection, subtract from selection and intersect with selection) and also for the amount of Feathering to be applied. This determines how much around the edge of the selection is slightly blurred, to give a soft-focus effect. The Marquee tools also have an option for setting a specific aspect for the selection, i.e. create it at a fixed ratio or size

The Marquee and Lasso tools are used to make selections by dragging the tool over the image. This can be symmetrical selections, e.g. Rectangular Marquee, or freehand, e.g. Lasso.

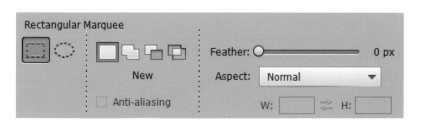

Menu Bar

In the Editor, the Menu bar contains menus that provide all of the functionality for the workings of Elements. Some of these functions can also be achieved through the use of the other components of Elements, such as the Toolbox, the Tool Options bar and the panels. However, the Menu bar is where all of the commands needed for the digital editing process can be accessed in one place.

Menu bar menus

- **File**. This has standard commands for opening, saving and printing images.

- **Edit**. This contains commands for undoing previous operations, and standard copy-and-paste techniques.

- **Image**. This contains commands for altering the size, shape and position of an image. It also contains more advanced functions, such as changing the color mode of an image.

- **Enhance**. This contains commands for editing the color elements of an image. It also contains quick-fix options and commands for creating Photomerge effects such as panoramas and combining exposures.

- **Layer**. This contains commands for working with different layers within an image.

- **Select**. This contains commands for working with areas that have been selected within an image, with one of the selection tools in the Toolbox.

- **Filter**. This contains numerous filters that can be used to apply special effects to an image.

- **View**. This contains commands for changing the size at which an image is displayed, and also options for showing or hiding rulers and grid lines.

- **Window**. This contains commands for changing the way multiple images are displayed, and also options for displaying the components of Elements.

- **Help**. This contains the various Help options.

Although the Menu bar menus are all available in each of the Editor modes, some of the menu options are not available in Quick edit or Guided edit mode.

Elements does not support the CMYK color model for editing digital images. This could be an issue if you use a commercial printer.

The Mac version of Elements also has a Photoshop Elements menu on the Menu bar. This contains the Preferences options.

20

Preferences

A number of preferences can be set within Elements to determine the way the program operates. It is perfectly acceptable to leave all of the default settings as they are, but as you become more familiar with the program you may want to change some of the preference settings. Preferences can be accessed by selecting **Edit > Preferences** from the Menu bar (**Adobe Photoshop Elements Editor > Preferences** in the Mac version). The available ones are:

- **General**. This contains a variety of options for selecting items, such as shortcut keys.

- **Saving Files**. This determines the way Elements saves files.

- **Performance**. This determines how Elements allocates memory when processing editing tasks.

- **Scratch Disks**. This determines how Elements allocates disk space when processing editing tasks (scratch disks). If you require more memory for editing you can do this by allocating up to four scratch disks. These act as extra areas from which memory can be used during editing.

- **Display & Cursors**. This determines how cursors operate when certain tools are selected.

- **Transparency**. This determines the color, or transparency, of the background on which an open image resides.

- **Units & Rulers**. This determines the unit of measurement used by items, such as rulers.

- **Guides & Grids**. This determines the color and format of any guides and grids that are used.

- **Plug-Ins**. This displays any plug-ins that have been downloaded to enhance image editing with Elements.

- **Adobe Partner Services** and **Update Options**. These can be used to check for related services and determine how updates to Elements are delivered.

- **Type**. This determines how text appears on images.

- **Country/Region Selection**. This is used to select your location from where you are using Elements.

Each preference has its own dialog box, in which the specific preference settings can be made.

A scratch disk is an area of temporary storage on the hard drive that can be utilized if the available memory (RAM) has been used up.

Guides and grids can be accessed from the View menu in Editor mode.

Organizer Workspace

The Organizer workspace contains functions for sorting, viewing and finding multiple images. To use the Organizer:

Images displayed in the Media View can be located from anywhere on your computer. The thumbnails in Media View are just references to the originals, wherever they are stored.

1 In any of the Editor modes, click on the **Organizer** button on the Taskbar

The Organizer has four views, in addition to eLive (see page 10), accessed from these buttons:

- Media View **Media**
- People View **People**
- Places View **Places**
- Events View **Events**

Media View

The Media View displays thumbnails of your photos, and also has functions for sorting and finding images:

Photos can be selected within the Organizer, and then opened in an Editor mode by clicking on this button on the Organizer Taskbar.

Editor

Folders and Albums   View buttons   Thumbnails

Organizer Taskbar   Instant Fix and Tag/Info buttons

Click on these buttons to apply image-editing effects to a selected image in Media View, or view the Tags and Information panels.

For information about using tags and keywords, see pages 46-47.

People View

This view can be used to tag specific people and then view photos with those people in them.

For information about using the Organizer, and its different views, see Chapter Two.

Places View

This view can be used to place photos on a map so that they can be searched for by location.

When you have a group of photos from the same location, add them to Places View so that this can be used to search over your photos.

Events View

This view can be used to group photos according to specific events such as birthdays and vacations.

Create Mode

Create mode is where you can release your artistic flair and start designing items such as photo books and photo collages. It can also be used to create slideshows, and to put your images onto discs. To use Create mode:

Use the Facebook Cover option to create a photo montage that is sized at the correct size to be used as your Facebook cover photo.

1 In either the Editor or the Organizer, click on the **Create** button

2 Select one of the Create projects. Each project has a wizard that takes you through the Create process. The projects include Photo Books, Greeting Cards, Photo Calendars, Photo Collages, cover photos for Facebook and covers for CDs/DVDs

Use your best 12 photos when using the Photo Calendar option.

3 The Create wizard takes you through the process so you can display your photos in a variety of creative ways

Making creations takes longer than normal image editing functions.

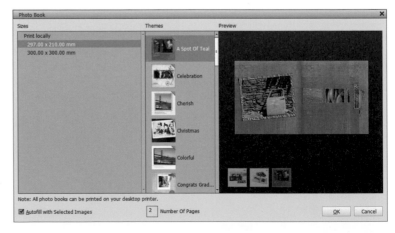

4 For most creations, there is a theme that can be applied, to which your own photos can then be added

5 Your photos can be added automatically from the Photo Bin, or you can drag them from there onto the creation

Click on the **Print** button once a creation has been made, to produce a hard copy.

6 Once your photos have been added a new file is created, to which you can add text, layout designs and graphics. Click on any available text boxes to add text there, click on the **Layouts** button to change the layout of the creation, and click on the **Graphics** button to add a background

Click on the **Save** button to save a completed creation in a specific file format, and the **Close** button to exit Create mode without saving the project.

7 Click on the **Advanced Mode** button to access the Expert Mode Toolbox, which can be used to edit the creation in the same way as for a standard photo

Advanced Mode

Share Mode

Share mode can be used to distribute your images to family and friends in a number of creative ways. To use Share mode:

1 In the Organizer, click on the **Share** button

2 Select one of the Share options, such as sharing to social media sites, sharing via email or creating a DVD or PDF Slideshow

Beware

The Share function can also be accessed from within the Editor, but there are fewer share options available.

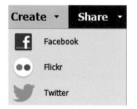

3 If you are sharing to email, the selected item is added to a wizard that can be used to determine the size and quality of the attachment that you want to send. Click on the **Next** button to move through the wizard

Beware

To share an image in an email you need to have an appropriate email app on your computer and an internet connection.

4 For sharing to social media sites, such as Facebook, Flickr and Twitter, Elements

has to initially be authorized to share content to these sites. Click on the **Authorize** button to give Elements permission to share to the selected app

There is always some risk in giving websites authorization to access your computer.

5 Enter your login details for the selected site and click on the **Authorise app** button (note that the spellings are localized)

You have to already have an account with a specific social media site in order to authorize Elements to use it; you cannot create an account during this process.

6 In the Elements window, click on the **Done** button to give Elements permission to share with the selected app

You only have to authorize Elements to use a social media site once. After that, photos can be shared in two clicks from the **Share** menu.

7 Once permission has been given for a social media site, you can share photos to the site by clicking on

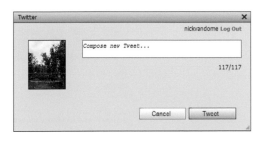

the **Share** button at the top of the Elements window, selecting the required app and entering the necessary information, i.e. a caption

27

Getting Help

One of the differences between Elements and the full version of Photoshop is the amount of assistance and guidance offered by each program. Since Photoshop is aimed more at the professional end of the market, the level of help is confined largely to the standard help directory, which serves as an online manual. Elements also contains this, but in addition it has the Getting Started option which is designed to take users through the digital image editing process as smoothly as possible. The Getting Started option offers general guidance about digital imaging techniques and there are also help items that can be accessed by selecting Help from the Menu bar. These include online help, information on available plug-ins for Elements, tutorials and support details.

Using the help files

eLive is a function in Elements 14 that provides a selection of tutorials and videos for getting the most out of Elements. To access these, click on the **eLive** button on the top toolbar in either Editor or Organizer mode.

1 Select **Photoshop Elements Help** from the **Help** menu and click on an item to display it in the main window. Use the left-hand panel to view the different help categories

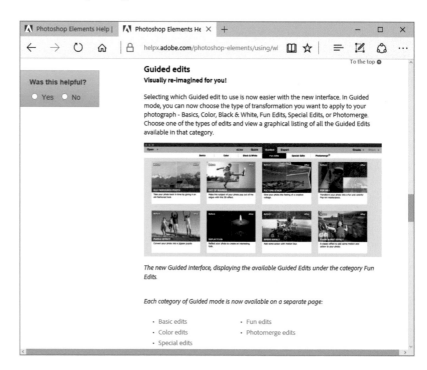

The keyboard shortcut for Photoshop Elements Help is F1.

2 Organizing Images

This chapter shows how to download digital images via Elements and then how to view and organize them, including using the People, Places and Events views. It shows how you can tag images, so that they are easy to find, how to search for items according to a variety of criteria, and also using albums and folders.

Obtaining Images

One of the first tasks in Elements is to import images so that you can start editing and sharing them. This can be done from a variety of devices, but the process is similar for all of them. To import images into Elements:

For many digital cameras, the Photo Downloader window will appear automatically once the camera is connected to the computer. However, if this does not happen, it will have to be accessed manually as shown here.

1 Access the **Organizer** by clicking on this button in the Editor

Organizer

2 Select **File > Get Photos and Videos** from the Menu bar and select the type of device from which you want to load images into Elements, or

From Files and Folders...	Ctrl+Shift+G
From Camera or Card Reader...	Ctrl+G
From Scanner...	Ctrl+U
In Bulk...	

Hot tip

The keyboard shortcut for obtaining images from a camera or card reader is Ctrl + G (Command key + G on a Mac).

3 Click on the **Import** button and select one of the options for obtaining images

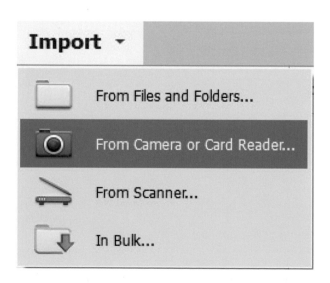

Hot tip

Images can also be imported from existing files and folders on a computer. This means that they will be added to the Organizer's database and you will be able to apply all of its features to the images.

4 If you select **From Camera or Card Reader**, click under **Get Photos from** to select a specific device. This can include directly from a digital camera (connected to your computer with a USB cable), a smartphone or a memory card, using a memory card reader

5 The images to be downloaded are displayed next to the device from which they will be downloaded

6 Click the **Browse** button to select a destination for the selected images

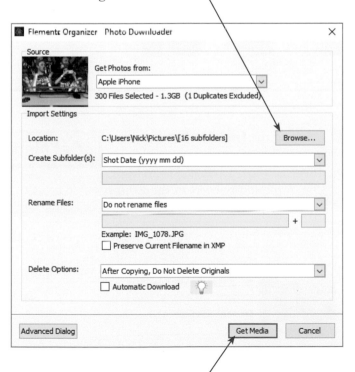

7 Click the **Get Media** button to download them

Images can also be downloaded from a USB flash drive. To do this, connect the flash drive and use the **From Camera or Card Reader** download option. You will then be able to download the images in the same way as with a camera or memory card reader.

The Delete Options box in the Photo Downloader has options for what happens once you have downloaded your photos. These are: **After Copying, Do Not Delete Originals**, **After Copying, Verify and Delete Originals** and **After Copying, Delete Originals**. If you do delete the originals from your camera or card reader, make sure you back up the ones that you have just downloaded, to an USB flash drive or an external hard drive.

...cont'd

8 Click on the **Advanced Dialog** button to access additional options for downloading your images. Here, you can select specific images so that they are not all downloaded at once

Hot tip

The Advanced Dialog Photo Downloader has an option to **Automatically Fix Red Eyes**. Check this box **On** if you want red eye to be removed from photos as they are downloaded.

32

Don't forget

Depending on the number of photos that you have on your camera or memory card, the downloading process may take a few minutes.

9 Click on the **Get Media** button so that the images are imported. They can then be viewed in the Organizer and opened in the Editor

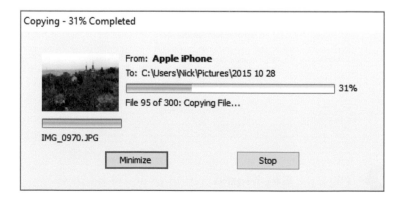

Hot tip

Click on the **Minimize** button in Step 9 so that you can get on with other tasks while your photos are being downloaded.

Importing in bulk

Using the Import function, it is also possible to import large numbers of images in one action, with the In Bulk option:

1 From the Organizer select **Import > In Bulk**

2 In the **Import Media** window you can select main folders to import, by checking the box next to them

3 Click here to select a subfolder

4 Check **Off** the main folder to deselect all subfolders

5 Click on a specific subfolder to select it. The main folder is also selected

6 Click on the **Import** button to import the selected folders

By default, the main top level folder (Pictures) is selected, and so are all of the subfolders.

Click on this button next to a folder (or subfolder) to add the folder to a Watch List. This means that when new images are added to this folder on your computer, they will automatically be imported by Elements.

Even though the main folder becomes selected in Step 5, only one sub-folder is selected. This is shown at the top right-hand side of the window.

Media View

Media View is the function within the Organizer that is used to view, find and sort images. When using Media View, images have to be actively added to it so it can then catalog them. Once images have been imported, Media View acts as a window for viewing and sorting your images, no matter where they are located. Media View is the default view when you access the Organizer and can be accessed at any time by clicking on the Media button:

To change the way images are displayed in Media View, select **View** from the Menu bar and check On or Off the **Details** option.

Media View can also be used to display video files, audio files, Elements' projects and PDF files. To view these, select **View > Media Types** from the Menu bar and check On the required items.

Folders and Albums

Tag and Info panels

Organizer Taskbar   Instant Fix and Tag Keyword/Info buttons

There is also a magnification slider on the Taskbar, which can be used for changing the size at which images are viewed in the main Media View window:

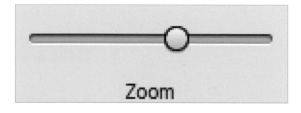

34

Accessing images

To access images within Media View:

1 Click on images to select them individually, or as a group

2 Drag here to scroll through images within the main window

3 Double-click on an image to view it in the whole Media View window

Hot tip

Select an image in the Organizer and select **View > Full Screen** from the Menu bar to view the image at the full size of your monitor.

Hot tip

To select multiple images, drag around the thumbnails, or hold down **Shift** and click on a range of thumbnails to select them all. Alternatively, hold down **Ctrl** (**Command** on a Mac) and click on thumbnails to select a group of non-consecutive images.

Hot tip

If images were captured with a digital camera, they will appear in Media View on the date the image was taken. To make sure this is accurate, set your camera to the correct date and time.

Media View can be set to watch specific folders on your computer. Whenever images are added to these folders, or edited within them, you will be prompted to add them into the Media View. To specify folders to be watched, select **File > Watch Folders** from the Menu bar and then browse to the folder, or folders, that you want to include.

If you use the Slideshow option and do not select any images, the whole catalog will be used for the slideshow.

When an Instant Fix is applied to a photo, a new photo is automatically created and this is stored within a **Version Set** with the original photo. See page 39 for more details on Version Sets.

...cont'd

Media View functionality

Media View has a considerable amount of power and functionality in terms of organizing and editing images within the Organizer. This includes the Taskbar and panels for adding tags to images, and viewing information about them:

1 The Taskbar is located at the bottom of the main window and contains buttons for, from left to right, show or hide the Albums and Folders panel, undo the previous action, rotate a selected image, tag people for People View, add images to a map for Places View, add an event to images for Event View, view the selected images in a slideshow, and access the selected images in the Editor

2 At the right-hand side of the Taskbar, use these buttons to apply editing fixes to a selected image and access the **Tags** and **Information** panels

3 Select an image in the main Media View window and click on this button to apply instant editing fixes to it (without having to move to the Editor)

4 Click on one of the editing functions to apply it to the select image(s)

5 Click on this button to view details of selected images in Media View

6 Click on the **Information** tab. Click on these arrows to expand each section

For more details about adding tags to images see pages 46-47.

7 Access the **General** panel to see information about the image name, size, date taken and where it is saved on your computer. You can edit the name and add a caption here

A caption can also be added to an image by selecting it and selecting **Edit > Add Caption** from the Menu bar.

37

8 Access the **Metadata** panel to see detailed information about an image that is added by the camera when it is taken

Metadata is information about an image that is stored in the image file itself, in addition to the image that is displayed.

9 Click on this button to view an expanded list of Metadata information

10 Access the **History** panel to view the editing history of the image

Stacks

Since digital cameras make it quick, easy and cheap to capture dozens, or hundreds of images on a single memory card, it is no surprise that most people are now capturing more images than ever before. One result of this is that it is increasingly tempting to take several shots of the same subject, just to try to capture the perfect image. The one drawback with this is that when it comes to organizing your images on a computer, it can become time-consuming to work your way through all of your near-identical shots. Media View offers a useful solution to this by allowing you to stack similar images, so that you can view a single thumbnail rather than several. To do this:

You can remove images from a stack by selecting the stack in Media View and selecting **Edit > Stack > Flatten Stack** from the Menu bar. However, this will remove all of the images, apart from the top one, from Media View. This does not remove them from your hard drive, although there is an option to do this too, if you wish.

To revert stacked images to their original state, select the stack and select **Edit > Stack > Unstack Photos** from the Menu bar.

Only stack similar photos, otherwise you may forget which photos are underneath the stack.

1 Select the images that you want to stack in Media View

2 Select **Edit > Stack > Stack Selected Photos** from the Menu bar

3 The images are stacked into a single thumbnail and the existence of the stack is indicated by this icon

4 To view all of the stacked images, click this button

5 Click here to return to all of the photos in Media View

Version Sets

When working with digital images it is commonplace to create several different versions from a single image. This could be to use one for printing and one for use on the web, or because there are elements of an image that you want to edit. Instead of losing track of images that have been edited, it is possible to create stacked thumbnails of edited images, which are known as Version Sets. These can include the original image and all of the edited versions. Version Sets can be created and added to from the Photo Editor and viewed in Media View. To do this:

1 Open an image in the Photo Editor

2 Make editing changes to the image in either Expert edit mode or Quick edit mode

3 Select **File > Save As** from the Menu bar

4 Check on the **Save in Version Set with Original** box and click **Save**

☑ Save in Version Set with Original

5 In Media View, the original image and the edited one are grouped together in a stack, and the fact that it is a Version Set is denoted next to the set

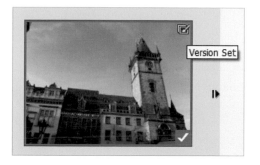

6 To view all of the images in a Version Set, select the set and select **Edit > Version Set > Expand Items in Version Set** from the Menu bar

The other Version Set menu options include **Flatten Version Set**, and **Revert to Original**. The latter deletes all of the other versions except the original image.

39

Version Sets are also created if an image has an Instant Fix applied to it in the Organizer.

People View

Shots of people are popular in most types of photography. However, this can result in hundreds, or thousands of photos of different people. In Elements there is a feature that enables you to tag people throughout your collections. This is known as People Recognition. To use this:

1 In the Organizer, click on the **People** button. Click on the **Named** button

2 Any named people are shown in the **Named** window

3 Click on the **Unnamed** button to view faces that have not already been assigned names

4 Click on one of the thumbnails to add a name

5 Add a name and click on the check mark symbol to apply the name to that group of photos

...cont'd

Adding people manually

To add names manually:

1 Open a photo at full size in Media View and click on the **Mark Face** button

Mark Face

2 A prompt box appears on the screen. Drag this over the required face, add a name in the **Add Name** box and click on the green check mark to apply the name

Viewing people

To view people who have been tagged with People Recognition:

1 Click on the **People** button in the main Organizer window

People

2 Click on the **Named** button. The people photos are stacked in a thumbnail. Click on the thumbnail to view all of the photos of that person (that have been tagged)

People Recognition really comes into its own when you have tagged dozens, or hundreds of photos. You can then view all of the photos containing a specific person.

The People View has been enhanced in Elements 14. You can now search using individual names.

Double-click on the thumbnails in the Named window to view the images in a grid. In the grid, double-click on a single image to view it at full size.

41

Places View

One of the most common reasons for taking photos is when people are on vacation in different and new locations. Within the Organizer it is possible to tag photos to specific locations on a map, so that you can quickly view all of your photos from a certain area. To do this:

1 In Media View, select all of the photos from a specific location

Hot tip

You can move around the map by clicking and dragging. You can also zoom in and out by right-clicking on the map and selecting the relevant command.

2 On the Taskbar, click on the **Add Location** button

3 Enter a location for the set of photos and click on the **Apply** button

4 To view photos that have been placed on a map, click on the **Places** button in the main Organizer window

Hot tip

Click on the **Unpinned** button at the top of the Places window to view all of the photos that have not had locations added to them. They appear next to the map so that they can be dragged onto a location.

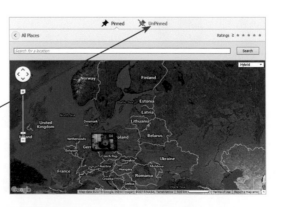

5 Use these controls to move around the map and zoom in and out on it

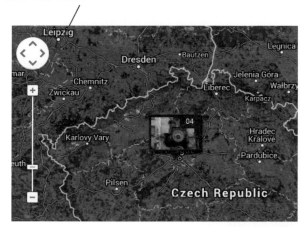

Hot tip

The map can be viewed as **Map**, **Hybrid**, **Light** or **Dark**. If **Map** is selected, there is also an option for viewing **Terrain**.

6 Click on a set of photos in a location. Click on this button to move through them

43

7 Double-click on a set of photos to view the individual photos in the left-hand panel

Beware

If a photo with an existing location is selected and the **Add Location** button is clicked, the location for the photo can be changed, but it will be removed from the original one.

8 Click on the **Done** button to exit the map   Done

Events View

Photos in the Organizer can also be allocated to specific events such as family celebrations or overseas trips. This is done with the Events View. To do this:

1 In Media View, select all of the required photos for a specific event

2 On the Taskbar, click on the **Add Event** button

3 In the **Add New Event** panel, add details including name, start and end date, and a description of the event

4 Click on the **Done** button

5 To view photos that have been allocated to an event, click on the **Events** button in the main Organizer window

6 All photos for a specific event are grouped together

44

7 Double-click on the thumbnail to view all of the photos allocated to the event

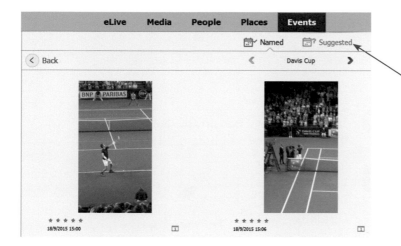

Click on the **Suggested** button at the top of the Events window to view groups of photos that Elements thinks may be suitable for new events.

8 Click on the **Back** button to go back to the thumbnail view in Step 6

9 Click on the **Calendar** to view events from specific dates

Calendar		Clear
	All Years ▼	
Jan	Feb	Mar
Apr	May	Jun
Jul	Aug	Sep
Oct	Nov	Dec

Right-click on an event thumbnail to access a menu with options to edit the event, remove it, set it as a cover photo for the event thumbnail, or view it as a slideshow.

10 Click on the **Add Event** button to create another event in Event View. This is done by dragging photos into the media bin and entering the event details as in Step 3

Add Event

Tagging Images

As your digital image collection begins to grow on your computer, it is increasingly important to be able to keep track of your images and find the ones you want, when you want them. One way of doing this is by assigning specific tags to images. You can then search for images according to the tags that have been added to them. The tagging function is accessed from the Tags panel within Media View in the Organizer. To add tags to images:

Hot tip

When you create a new category you can also choose a new icon.

NEW

46

Tags can also be created for People, Places and Events. These are also created when items are added to the various sections. This is a new feature in Elements 14.

Don't forget

Tags are also referred to as Keywords or Keyword tags.

1 In Media View, click on this button on the Taskbar to show and hide the Tags panel

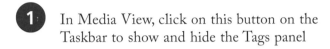

2 Click here to access the currently-available tags

3 Click here to access sub-categories for a particular category

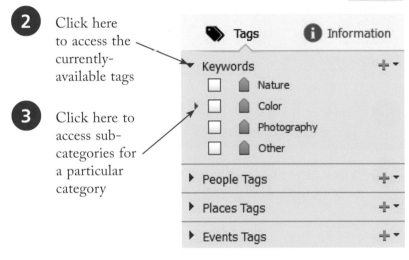

4 Click here to add categories, or sub-categories, of your own choice

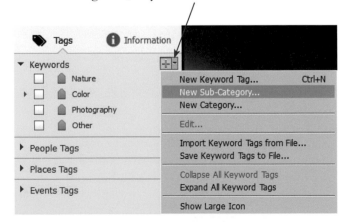

5 Enter a name for the new category, or sub-category, and click on the **OK** button

Create Sub-Category ✕

Sub-Category Name
Travel

Parent Category or Sub-Category
Photography ▼

OK   Cancel

6 Select the required images from Media View

7 Drag a tag onto one of the selected images

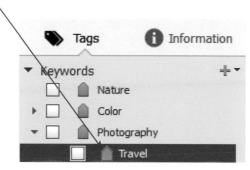

🏷 Tags   ℹ Information

▼ Keywords   ＋▾
  ☐ 🔖 Nature
▸ ☐ 🔖 Color
▼ ☐ 🔖 Photography
    ☐ 🔖 Travel

8 The tag will apply to all of the selected images. Each individual image will have the tag added to it

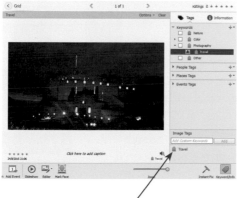

9 The images are tagged with the icon that denotes the main category, rather than the sub-category

Hot tip

Multiple tags can be added to the same image. This gives you greater flexibility when searching for images.

Don't forget

Categories can have several levels of sub-categories. To create additional levels, right-click on a sub-category and select **Create new Sub-Category** from the menu. Give the sub-category a name and ensure that the required item is selected in the **Parent Category or Sub-Category** box.

Don't forget

Tagged images can still be searched for by using a sub-category tag, even though they are denoted in Media View by the tag for the main category.

Searching for Images

Once images have been tagged, they can then be searched for using those specific tags. To do this:

Using the Search box

Images can be searched for simply by typing keywords into the Search box at the top of the Organizer, in any view:

1 Click in the Search box

2 Enter a keyword. As you type, suggestions will appear, including items that have been added to People View, Places View and Events View

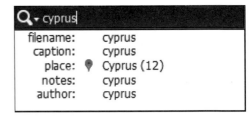

3 Click on one of the results to view all of the tagged images

4 Click on the **Back** button to go back to all of the images

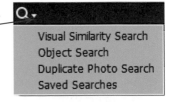

5 Click here in the Search box to access other search options

Searching with tags

Images can also be searched for by using the tags within the Tags panel. To do this:

1 Access the Tags panel from this button

2 Check on a box to view the images that are tagged with that keyword

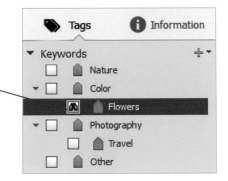

3 All matching items for a search are shown together within the Media View window

4 Click on the **All Media** button to return to the rest of the images

Tags can be viewed for **Keywords**, **People Tags**, **Places Tags** and **Events Tags**. This is a new feature in Elements 14.

If you search using a main category, any items that are within that category as a sub-category will be searched for too. If you select a sub-category, this is only what will be searched for.

Rollover a tag next to a photo in Media View to see a description of the keyword tag.

...cont'd

Multiple searches

Within the Tags panel it is also possible to define searches for images that have multiple (i.e. two or more) tags attached to them. To do this:

1 Add a tag to an image or images, and click on the tag in the Tags panel to display all of these images (other tags that have been added to them will also be displayed next to the image)

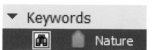

2 Add another tag to the image or images, so that there are at least two attached. Click on both of these in the Tags panel. Only the images containing both tags will be displayed

Searching for people

Tags can be added to people in the same way as for adding them to any other items. Also, if people have been tagged using the People Recognition tool in the People section of the Organizer (see pages 40-41) these tags will be added in the Tags section of the Organizer. To search for people:

1 In the Organizer, click on this button

Keyword/Info

NEW

Searching for people using tags is a new feature in Elements 14.

2 Click on the right-pointing triangle next to **People Tags** to expand this panel

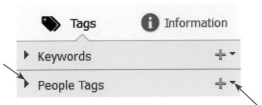

Tags · Information
▶ Keywords · +▾
▶ People Tags · +▾

Hot tip

New people names, and also group names, can be added to the People Tags by clicking here and selecting **New Person** or **New Group**.

3 Tags that have been added in the People section are displayed

▼ People Tags · +▾
☐ 👤 Eilidh
☐ 👤 Lucy
☐ 👤 Nick
☐ 👥 Colleagues
☐ 👥 Family
☐ 👥 Friends

51

4 Click next to a person to view the images that have been tagged with their name

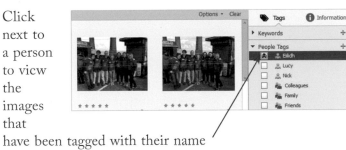

Beware

The more people tags that are selected, the fewer the number of results that will be returned.

5 Select another tag to view images that have two (or more) people in them

▶ Keywords
▼ People Tags
☑ 👤 Eilidh
☐ 👤 Lucy
☑ 👤 Nick
☐ 👥 Colleagues

Albums

Albums in Elements are similar to physical photo albums: they are a location into which you can store all of your favorite groups of images. Once they have been stored there, they can easily be found when required. To create albums:

Version Sets and Stacks can be added to and viewed in Albums.

1 In Media View, click here in the Albums panel and select **New Album**

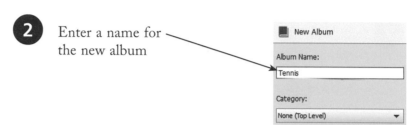

2 Enter a name for the new album

Click on the New Album button in Step 1 to view options for collapsing or expanding all of the albums in the panel.

3 Select the images that you would like included in the new album and drag them into the Content panel

Right-click on an album name to access a menu with options to **Edit**, **Rename** or **Delete** the album.

4 Click on the **OK** button

5 The selected images are placed into the new album. Click on an album to view the images within it

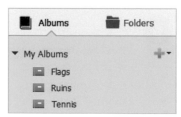

Folders

One important factor in storing and searching for photos is the use of folders. Elements can replicate the folder structure that you have on your hard drive and also create new folders and edit existing ones. To work with folders in Elements:

1 The available folders are listed next to the Albums section. Click on a folder to view its contents

2 New folders are created whenever you import photos into Elements using the **Import > From Files and Folders** command

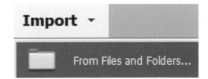

3 In hierarchy view, right-click on a folder to access the available options for editing it or adding a new folder

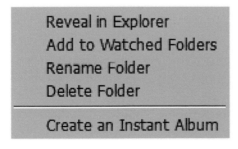

Don't forget

Even if you import a single photo, the related folder will be created within Elements, containing the photo.

Hot tip

Right-click within the hierarchy view to add a new folder. When this is completed it also appears within your file structure on your computer's hard drive.

Opening and Saving Images

Once you have captured images with a digital camera or a scanner, and stored them on your computer, you can open them in any of the Editor modes. There are a number of options for this:

Open command

1 Select **File > Open** from the Menu bar or click on the **Open** button and select an option

2 Select an image from your hard drive and click **Open**

Open As command

This can be used to open a file in a different file format to its original. To do this:

1 Select **File > Open As** from the Menu bar

2 Select an image and select the file format. Click **Open**

Saving images

When saving digital images, it is always a good idea to save them in at least two different file formats, particularly if layered objects such as text and shapes have been added. One of these formats should be the proprietary Photoshop format PSD or PDD. The reason for using this is that it will retain all of the layered information within an image. So, if a text layer has been added, it will still be available for editing once it has been saved and closed.

The other format that an image should be saved in, is the one most appropriate for the use to which it is going to be put. Therefore, images that are going to be used on the web should be saved as JPEG, GIF or PNG files, while an image that is going to be used for printing should be saved in another format, such as TIFF. Once images have been saved in these formats, all of the layered information within them becomes flattened into a single layer and it will not be possible to edit these individual layers.

Hot tip

Another option for opening files is the **Open Recently Edited File** command, which is accessed from the File menu. This lists, in order, the files you have opened most recently. Some of these are also listed on the **Open** button's drop-down menu.

Don't forget

A proprietary file format is one that is specific to the program being used. It has greater flexibility when used within the program itself, but cannot be distributed as easily as other images.

Don't forget

The **Save As** command should be used if you want to make a copy of an image with a different file name.

54

Working with Video

As well as using Elements for viewing and organizing photos, it can also be used in the same way with video. Video can be imported into Elements in a number of ways:

- From a camera that has video recording capabilities

- From a digital video camera

- From a cell/mobile phone

- From video that has been created in the Elements Premiere program. This is a companion program to Elements and is used to manipulate and edit video. It can be bought in a package with Elements, or individually. For more details see **www.adobe.com/products/premiere-elements/**

Elements Premiere can be bought as a package with Elements, or it can be bought individually.

To download video into Elements:

1 Connect the device containing the video. In the Organizer, click on the **Import** button, select the required device and download in the same way as for photos

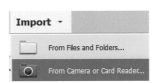

2 The video is downloaded and displayed in the Organizer, in the same way as photos

Video files are usually much larger in size than photos, and if you have lots of them they will take up a lot of space on your computer.

3 Video clips are identified by this symbol on their thumbnail in Media View in the Organizer

...cont'd

Viewing video

To view video clips:

Beware

Most videos captured on smartphones and digital video cameras will play in Elements, but some that are captured with special effects, such as slow-motion, may not.

1 Double-click on the clip in Media View. The Elements video player will open and play the video clip

2 Use the controls underneath the video window to adjust the volume using the slider control to the left, and navigate through the clip using the **Rewind**, **Play/Pause** and **Fast Forward** buttons

Don't forget

The **Find > By Media Type** option can also be used to find audio files, projects and PDFs.

Finding video

To find video clips within Elements:

1 In the Organizer, select **Find > By Media Type > Video** from the Menu bar, and the video files will be displayed

Hot tip

The keyboard shortcut for viewing video by media type is Alt + 2.

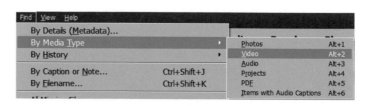

3 First Digital Steps

This chapter shows how to get up and running with digital image editing, and details some effective editing techniques for improving digital images, such as improving the overall color and duplicating items.

Color Enhancements

Some of the simplest, but most effective editing changes that can be made to digital images are color enhancements. These can help to transform a mundane image into a stunning one, and Elements offers a variety of methods for achieving this. Some of these are verging towards the professional end of image editing, while others are done almost automatically by Elements. These are known as Auto adjustments, and some simple manual adjustments can also be made to the brightness and contrast of an image. All of these color enhancement features can be accessed from the Enhance menu on the Menu bar, in both Expert and Quick edit modes.

Auto Levels

This automatically adjusts the overall color tone of an image in relation to the lightest and darkest points in the image:

Auto Contrast

This automatically adjusts the contrast of an image:

...cont'd

Auto Color Correction

This automatically adjusts all of the color elements within an image:

The keyboard shortcut for Auto Color Correction is Shift + Ctrl + B (Shift + Command key + B on a Mac).

Adjust Brightness/Contrast

This can be used to manually adjust the brightness and contrast in an image:

1 Select **Enhance > Adjust Lighting > Brightness/Contrast** from the Menu bar (in either Expert or Quick edit mode)

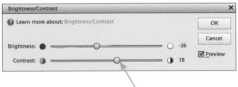

Alter the Brightness and Contrast by small amounts at a time when you are editing an image. This will help ensure that the end result does not look too unnatural.

2 Drag the sliders to adjust the image's brightness and contrast

3 Click on the **OK** button

4 The brightness and contrast (and a range of other color editing functions) can also be adjusted using the panels in Quick edit mode

Always make sure that the Preview box is checked when you are applying color enhancements. This will display the changes as you make them, and before they are applied to the image.

59

...cont'd

Hot tip

Adjusting shadows can make a significant improvement to an image in which one area is under-exposed and the rest is correctly exposed.

Don't forget

Shadows and Highlights can also be adjusted in the Levels panel: **Enhance > Adjust Color > Levels** from the Menu bar. See pages 108-111 for more details about Levels.

Beware

Some digital cameras have a tendency to create slightly darker images, so adjusting the Shadows/Highlights is always a good option.

Adjust Shadows/Highlights

One problem that most photographers encounter at some point, is where part of an image is exposed correctly, while another part is either over- or under-exposed. If this is corrected using general color correction techniques, such as adjusting levels of brightness and contrast, the poorly-exposed area may be improved, but at the expense of the area that was correctly exposed initially. To overcome this, the Shadows/Highlights command can be used to adjust particular tonal areas of an image. To do this:

1 Open an image where parts of the image, or all of it, are incorrectly exposed

2 Select **Enhance > Adjust Lighting > Shadows/ Highlights** from the Menu bar

3 Make the required adjustments by dragging the sliders

4 Click on the **OK** button

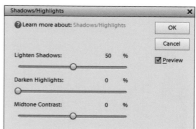

5 The poorly-exposed areas of the image have been corrected

Cropping

Cropping is a technique that can be used to remove unwanted areas of an image and highlight the main subject. The area to be cropped can only be selected as a rectangle. To crop an image:

1 Select the **Crop** tool from the Toolbox

2 Click and drag on an image to select the area to be cropped. The area that is selected is retained and the area to be cropped appears grayed-out

3 Click and drag on these markers to resize the crop area

4 Click on the check mark to accept the changes, or the circle to reject them

Don't forget

Most photos benefit from some cropping, to give the main subject more prominence.

Hot tip

The Tool Options for the Crop tool have an option for selecting pre-set sizes for the Crop tool. This results in the crop being in specific proportions. For instance, if you want to print an image at 10 x 8 size, you can use this pre-set crop size to ensure that the cropped image has the correct proportions. The image dialog box will also be updated accordingly.

...cont'd

Overlay crop options

When cropping photos it is also possible to use various overlay grids to help the composition of the image. One of these is the Rule of Thirds. This is a photographic technique where a nine-segment grid is used to position elements within the image. Generally, the items that you want to give the most prominence to should be positioned at one of the intersections of the lines. To use the Rule of Thirds grid:

Don't forget

The different crop options are all accessed from the Tool Options bar, with the Crop tool selected.

1 Select the **Crop** tool and click on the **Rule of Thirds** button in the Tool Options panel

Grid Overlay:

2 Crop the image so that at least one of the main subjects is located at the intersections of the lines in the grid. This can be in the foreground or the background

3 The image is cropped according to the Rule of Thirds grid

Auto Crop

To simplify the crop function, Elements 14 also has a range of auto crop options, where the suggested crop area is displayed using a range of preset options. To use these:

Don't forget

Images can also be cropped using a larger grid. This can be useful if you are trying to align items within an image.

1 Select the **Crop** tool. The auto crop options are displayed on four buttons in the Tool Options panel

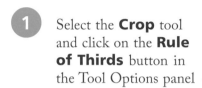

2 Move the cursor over one of the options to view the auto crop selection

3 The auto crop selection is shown in the main window. Click on the green check mark to accept the suggested crop area, or click on the red circle to reject the suggestion

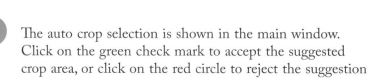

Healing Brush

One of the most popular techniques in digital imaging is removing unwanted items, particularly physical blemishes such as spots and wrinkles. This can be done with the Clone tool but the effects can sometimes be too harsh, as a single area is copied over the affected item. A more subtle effect can be achieved with the Healing Brush and the Spot Healing Brush tools. The Healing Brush can be used to remove blemishes over larger areas, such as wrinkles:

1 Open an image with blemishes covering a reasonably large area, i.e. more than a single spot

2 Select the **Healing Brush** tool from the Toolbox and make the required selections in the Tool Options bar

3 Hold down **Alt** and click on an area of the image to load the Healing Brush tool. Drag over the affected area. The cross is the area which is copied beneath the circle. At this point the overall tone is not perfect and looks too pink

4 Release the mouse, and the Healing Brush blends the affected area with the one that was copied over it. This creates a much more natural skin tone

The Healing Brush tool can be more subtle than the Clone tool, as it blends the copied area together with the area over which it is copying. This is particularly effective on images of people, as it preserves the overall skin tone better than the Clone tool does.

The Spot Healing Brush tool can be used to remove items such as small blemishes or spots. Click on this button in the Healing Brush Tool Options bar and drag it over the affected area to remove it.

When dragging over a blemish with the Spot Healing Brush tool, make sure the brush size is larger than the area of the blemish. This will ensure that you can cover the blemish in a single stroke.

If you are copying a large object with cloning, do not release the mouse once you have started dragging the cursor during the cloning process, otherwise the cloned image will be incomplete.

Hot tip

Cloning is a fun way to create instant twins.

Hot tip

When you are removing large objects by cloning you will probably have to move your source point several times. This will ensure that there is smooth coverage of the cloned item.

Cloning

Cloning is a technique that can be used to copy one area of an image over another. This can be used to cover up small imperfections in an image, such as a dust mark or a spot, and also to copy or remove large items in an image, such as a person.

To clone items:

1 Select the **Clone Stamp** tool from the Toolbox

2 Set the Clone Stamp options in the Tool Options bar

3 Hold down Alt, and then click on the image to select a source point from which the cloning will start

4 Drag the cursor to copy everything over which the selection point marker passes

Pattern Cloning

The Pattern Stamp tool can be used to copy a selected pattern over an image, or onto a selected area of an image. To do this:

1 Select the **Pattern Stamp** tool from the Toolbox

2 Click here in the Tool Options bar to access the available patterns

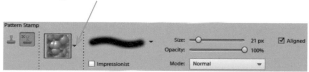

3 Select a pattern for the Pattern Stamp tool

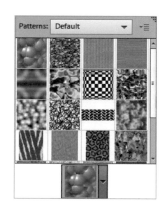

4 Click and drag on an image to copy the selected pattern over it

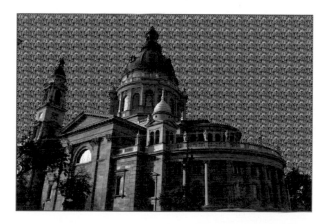

Rotating

Various rotation commands can be applied to images, and also individual layers in layered images. This can be useful for positioning items and also for correcting the orientation of an image that is on its side or upside down.

Rotating a whole image

For more information about working with layers, see Chapter Eight.

1 Select **Image > Rotate** from the Menu bar

2 Select a rotation option from the menu

3 Select **Custom** to enter your own value for the amount you want an image rotated

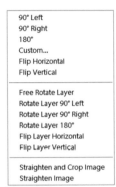

90° Left
90° Right
180°
Custom...
Flip Horizontal
Flip Vertical

Free Rotate Layer
Rotate Layer 90° Left
Rotate Layer 90° Right
Rotate Layer 180°
Flip Layer Horizontal
Flip Layer Vertical

Straighten and Crop Image
Straighten Image

If an image is only slightly misaligned, then only a small angle value is required in the **Rotate Canvas** dialog box. A figure of 1 or 2 can sometimes be sufficient.

Rotate Canvas

Angle: 5   ● °Right   OK
            ○ °Left   Cancel

4 Click the **OK** button

OK

Rotating a layer
To rotate separate layers within an image:

Images can also be rotated using the **Straighten** tool in the Toolbox. To do this, drag the tool on the image to create the required effect.

1 Open an image that consists of two or more layers. Select one of the layers in the Layers panel

2 Select **Image > Rotate** from the Menu bar

3 Select a layer rotation option from the menu

4 The selected layer is rotated independently

Transforming

The Transform commands can be used to resize an image, and to apply some basic distortion techniques. These commands can be accessed by selecting **Image > Transform** from the Menu bar.

Free Transform

This enables you to manually alter the size and shape of an image. To do this:

1 Select **Image > Transform > Free Transform** from the Menu bar

2 Click and drag here to transform the vertical and horizontal size of the image. Hold down **Shift** to transform it in proportion

Hot tip

Click just outside this placeholder and drag left or right to manually rotate an image with the Transform function.

Don't forget

The other options from the Transform menu are Skew, Distort and Perspective. These can be accessed and applied in a similar way to the Free Transform option.

Magnification

In Elements, there are a number of ways in which the magnification at which an image is being viewed can be increased or decreased. This can be useful if you want to zoom in on a particular part of an image, for editing purposes, or if you want to view a whole image to see the result of editing effects that have been applied.

Don't forget

The View menu can be used to display rulers at the top and left of an image, which can be useful for precise measurements and placement. There is also a command for displaying a grid over the top of the whole image.

View menu

1 Select **View** from the Menu bar and select one of the options from the View menu

View	Window	Help
New Window for bulgaria4.jpg		
Zoom In		Ctrl+=
Zoom Out		Ctrl+-
Fit on Screen		Ctrl+0
Actual Pixels		Ctrl+1
Print Size		
Selection		Ctrl+H
Rulers		Shift+Ctrl+R
Grid		Ctrl+'

Hot tip

The keyboard shortcut for zooming in is:
PC: Ctrl + =
Mac: Command key + =

The keyboard shortcut for zooming out is:
PC: Ctrl + -
MAC: Command key + -

Zoom tool

1 Select the **Zoom** tool from the Toolbox

2 Click once on an image to enlarge it (usually by 100% each time). Hold down **Alt** and click to decrease the magnification

Hot tip

Click and drag with the Zoom tool over a small area to increase the magnification to the maximum, i.e. 3200%. This can be particularly useful when performing close-up editing tasks, such as removing red-eye.

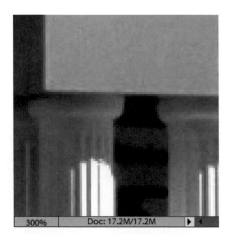

300%   Doc: 17.2M/17.2M

...cont'd

Navigator panel

This can be used to move around an image and also magnify certain areas. To use the Navigator panel:

1 Access the **Navigator** panel by selecting **Window > Navigator** from the Menu bar

The keyboard shortcut for accessing the Navigator panel is F12.

2 Drag this slider to magnify the area of the image within the red rectangle

Zoom: — ⬤ + 34.45%

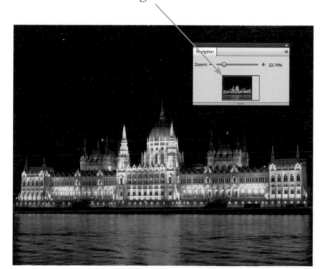

The Navigator also has buttons for zooming in and out. These are located at the left and right of the slider.

3 Drag the rectangle to change the area of the image that is being magnified

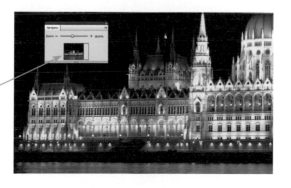

Click on different areas on the thumbnail in the Navigation panel to view these areas in the main Editor window.

Don't forget

The Background Eraser tool can be used to remove an uneven background. To do this, drag over the background with the Background Eraser tool and, depending on the settings in the Tool Options panel, everything that it is dragged over will be removed.

Don't forget

If the **Contiguous** box is not checked, the background color will be removed wherever it occurs in the image. If the Contiguous box is checked, the background color will only be removed where it touches another area of the same color, which is not broken by another element of the image.

Eraser

The Eraser tool can be used to remove areas of an image. In a simple, single layer image, this can just leave a blank hole, which has to be filled with something. The Eraser options are:

- **Eraser**, which can be used to erase part of the background image or a layer within it

- **Background Eraser**, which can be used to remove an uneven background

- **Magic Eraser**, which can be used to quickly remove a solid background (see below)

Erasing a background

With the Magic Eraser tool, it is possible to delete a colored background in an image. To do this:

1 Open an image with an evenly-colored background

2 Select the **Magic Eraser** and make the required selections in the Tool Options bar. Make sure the Contiguous box is not checked

3 Click once on the background. It is removed from the image, regardless of where it occurs

4 Quick Wins

This chapter looks at some of the "quick wins" that can be done in Elements, such as removing unwanted objects, changing photos to black and white, and improving hazy photos. It also shows some of the Guided and Quick edit options that provide step-by-step actions for creating a range of creative and striking photos.

Removing Red-Eye

One of the most common problems with photographs of people, whether they are taken digitally or with a film-based camera, is red-eye. This is caused when the camera's flash is used, and then reflects in the subject's pupils. This can create the dreaded red-eye effect, when the subject can unintentionally be transformed into a demonic character.

Elements has recognized that removing red-eye is one of the top priorities for most amateur photographers, and a specific tool for this purpose has been included in the Toolbox: the Red Eye Removal tool. This is available in Expert or Quick edit modes:

The best way to deal with red-eye is to avoid it in the first place. Try using a camera that has a red-eye reduction function.

Don't forget

There is also an option in the Red Eye Removal tool for removing red-eye from pets.

Don't forget

Red-eye can also be removed when images are being downloaded from the camera. This is an option in the Photo Downloader window.

Hot tip

Red-eye can be removed automatically by clicking on the **Auto Correct** button in the Red Eye Removal Tool Options panel.

1 Open an image that contains red-eye

2 Select the **Zoom** tool from the Toolbox

3 Drag around the affected area until it appears at a suitable magnification. Select the **Red Eye Removal** tool from the Toolbox

4 Click in the Tool Options bar to select the size of the pupil and the amount by which it will be darkened

| Pupil Radius: | 50% |
| Darken: | 50% |

5 Click once on the red-eye, or drag around the affected area to remove the red-eye

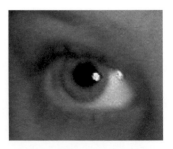

Red Eye Removal

Auto Correct

72

Changing to Black and White

Most digital cameras and scanners are capable of converting color images into black and white at the point of capture. However, it is also possible to use Elements to convert existing color images into black and white ones. To do this:

1 Open a color image and select **Enhance > Convert to Black and White** from the Menu bar

2 The Convert to Black and White dialog box has various options for how the image is converted

3 Select the type of black and white effect to be applied, depending on the subject in the image

4 Drag these sliders to specify the intensity of the effect to be applied for different elements

5 Click on the **OK** button

6 The image is converted into black and white, according to the settings that have been selected

The keyboard shortcut to access the Convert to Black and White dialog window is Alt + Ctrl + B (Alt + Command key + B on a Mac).

A similar effect can be achieved by selecting **Enhance > Adjust Color > Remove Color** from the Menu bar.

The Guided edits also have an option for turning photos into black and white: **Guided > Black & White > Black and White**.

Quickly Removing Items

One of the most annoying aspects of taking photos is to capture what you think is a perfect image, only to find that there is an unwanted object in the final shot. In Elements, it is possible to delete unwanted items and automatically fill-in the area from where these are removed. To do this:

Don't forget

Several different items can be removed from the same photo. To do this, select each one separately and perform the actions from Step 3 onwards, on these pages.

74

Hot tip

The selection around the object does not have to be too accurate, as long as it goes around the border of the object.

Beware

If an area is just selected and then deleted, it will leave a blank space, filled with either the color palette's background or foreground color.

 Open an image which contains an unwanted object

 Use one of the selection tools to select the unwanted object

Select **Edit > Fill Selection** from the Menu bar

Edit	Image	Enhance	Layer
Undo Lasso			Ctrl+Z
Redo Fill			Ctrl+Y
Revert			Shift+Ctrl+A
Cut			Ctrl+X
Copy			Ctrl+C
Copy Merged			Shift+Ctrl+C
Paste			Ctrl+V
Paste Into Selection			Shift+Ctrl+V
Delete			
Fill Selection...			

4 Make the selections in the Fill Layer dialog box. Ensure **Content-Aware** is selected in the **Contents** section

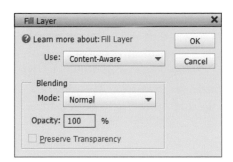

Fill Layer

ℹ Learn more about: Fill Layer

Use: Content-Aware ▾

OK

Cancel

Blending

Mode: Normal ▾

Opacity: 100 %

☐ Preserve Transparency

5 Click on the **OK** button

6 The selection is deleted and the area is automatically filled with the background

Beware

If there are too many colors around the selected area the fill effect may appear inaccurate. If this is the case, try with a slightly different selection area.

7 The final image makes it appear that the unwanted object was never there in the first place

Don't forget

Zoom in to the final image to make sure that the background has been filled as accurately as possible.

Moving Items in a Photo

Unless you are taking photos under studio conditions, it is probable that you will get some unwanted items in your photos, or the composition may not be exactly as you would like it in terms of the position of the subjects. The answer to this is the Content-Aware editing tool. This can be used to move subjects in a photo and then have the background behind them filled in automatically.

Hot tip

In the Content-Aware Move Options panel, drag the **Healing** slider to specify how the edited area blends with the rest of the image.

1 Open an image with a subject that you want to move

2 Select the **Content-Aware Move** tool from the Toolbox

3 Check on the **Move** box in Tool Options

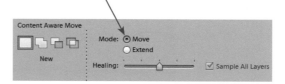

Don't forget

When moving items, it is most effective when the background has a reasonable amount of solid or similar colors.

4 Drag around the subject that you want to move

Hot tip

The Content-Aware Move selection area can be moved by using the arrow keys on the keyboard, e.g. left and right, up and down.

5 Drag the subject to a new position

6 The area where the subject was previously located is filled in by the Content-Aware function

The subject can be positioned anywhere in the photo.

The Content-Aware tool can also be used to extend areas within an image. To do this, check on the **Extend** box in Tool Options, drag around the area you want to extend and then drag the selection into place. The Content-Aware Move tool will automatically fill in the background for the area that is extended.

Removing Haze

Despite our best efforts, some photos do not come out the way we hoped. One problem can be that photos appear hazy, which is often accompanied by a washed-out sky. To remedy this:

Haze Removal is a new feature in Elements 14.

Haze reduction is a good option for landscape photos that have been taken in dull lighting.

Toggle the **Before/ After** button at the bottom of the Haze Removal window to view the two states of the image.

There is also an Auto Haze Removal option that can be accessed from the Menu bar in Expert or Quick edit mode: **Enhance > Auto Haze Removal**.

1 Open a photo that is suffering from a hazy effect

2 Select **Enhance > Haze Removal** from the Menu bar in Expert or Quick edit mode

3 The Haze Removal window displays the image

4 Drag this slider to apply the haze removal effect

5 Drag this slider to apply the degree of the effect

Improving Selfies

Selfies (self-portraits, usually taken with the front-facing camera on a smartphone) are one of the phenomena of modern life. Love them or loathe them, it is hard to get through a day without seeing someone pointing their phone at themselves to take a photo. One of the photographic problems with selfies is that they can be a bit blurred, due to the taker's arm shaking slightly as they hold the camera. To remedy this:

Shake Reduction is a new feature in Elements 14.

1 Open a photo of yourself that you think may be slightly blurred

There is also an Auto Shake Reduction option that can be accessed from the Menu bar in Expert or Quick edit mode: **Enhance > Auto Shake Reduction**.

2 Zoom in on the photo to check the focus

"Selfie Sticks" can be used to take photos of yourself, but these should be avoided if possible: they can get in the way of other people, and some areas and venues have banned them altogether.

3 Select **Enhance > Shake Reduction** from the Menu bar in Expert or Quick edit mode

4 The marker box is the area that is used to improve the focus. Drag this box to change the area, or drag on a corner to expand the area

Click on this button to draw a new marker box on the photo.

5 Drag on this slider to alter the intensity of the effect

Quick Edit Mode Options

The Quick edit options in Elements offer a number of functions within the one location. This makes it easier to apply a number of techniques at the same time.

Using Quick edit mode

There are some new additions within the Effects panel in Elements 14.

Quick edit mode is a good way to view how certain editing functions are applied automatically. Once you are confident with this, you can use Expert mode to perform similar tasks manually, which can give you more control over the final effects.

1 Open an image in the Editor and click on the **Quick** button

2 The Quick edit mode has a modified Toolbox, with fewer tools, that is displayed here

3 Click on bottom toolbar to access the Quick edit panel options. The default one is for **Adjustments**

4 Click on the **Adjustments** panel to make the appropriate changes (see pages 82-83)

The other Quick edit panels are: **Effects**, **Textures** and **Frames**. See pages 84-85 for more details.

Quick Edit Toolbox

The Quick edit Toolbox has a reduced Toolbox that includes:

- Zoom tool
- Hand tool
- Quick Selection tool
- Red-Eye Removal tool
- Whiten Teeth tool
- Straighten tool
- Text tool
- Spot Healing/Healing tool
- Crop tool
- Move tool

Hot tip

To show, or hide the Quick edit Toolbox (and also the Expert edit Toolbox) select **Window > Tools** from the Menu bar.

Whitening teeth

One of the tool options in the Quick edit mode Toolbox is for whitening teeth in a photo. To do this:

1 Open an image and click on the **Whiten Teeth** tool, and select a brush size for the tool

2 Drag the Whiten Teeth tool over the teeth

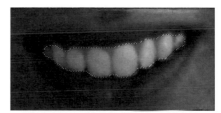

3 The teeth area is selected and whitened in one operation

Beware

The Red-Eye Removal tool is the same as the one in Expert mode, including the Pet Eye option for removing red-eye in photos of pets.

Beware

Do not overdo the teeth whitening effect, otherwise it will start to look unnatural.

Quick Edit Adjustments

The adjustment panels in the Quick edit section are:

Don't forget

Changes are displayed in the main Quick edit window, in real-time, as they are being made.

Smart Fix panel
This performs several editing changes in a single operation. Click on the Auto button to have the changes applied automatically, or drag the slider to specify the extent of the editing changes. Click on the thumbnails to apply preset amounts of the change.

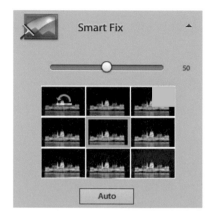

Hot tip

The Exposure panel is a good option for quickly editing photos that are under- or over-exposed, i.e. too dark or too light.

Exposure panel
This provides options for adjusting the lighting and contrast in an image. Drag the sliders to adjust the exposure, or click on one of the thumbnails to apply a preset option.

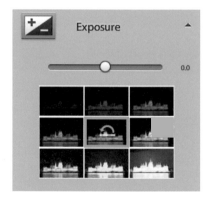

Don't forget

Shadows and highlights can be edited within Expert mode: **Enhance > Adjust Lighting > Shadows/Highlights**.

Lighting panel
This provides options for adjusting the lightest and darkest points in an image. This is done by adjusting the shadows, midtones and highlights. Drag the slider to adjust this or click on one of the thumbnails for an auto option.

Color panel

Click on the Auto button to automatically adjust the hue and saturation of an image, or drag the slider to make manual adjustments. Click on the thumbnails to apply preset amounts.

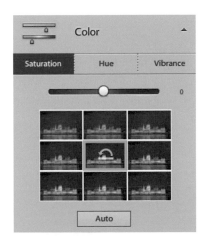

The Balance panel can be used to create some abstract color effects.

Balance panel

Drag the slider to adjust the warmth of the colors of an image and the color balance. Click on the thumbnails to apply preset amounts.

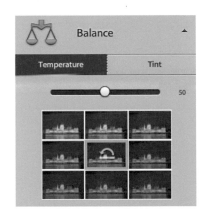

Sharpen panel

This can be used to apply sharpening to an image to make it clearer, either automatically with the Auto button, or the panel thumbnails, or manually with the slider.

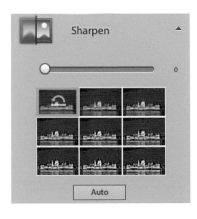

Sharpening works by increasing the contrast between adjoining pixels to make the overall image appear more in focus. It can also be accessed by selecting **Enhance > Auto Sharpen** or **Enhance > Unsharp Mask** from the Expert menu bar. The Unsharp Mask option has a dialog window where the effect can be added as a percentage.

Enhancing with Quick Edits

In addition to the Adjustments option, the other buttons on the Quick edit toolbar are for adding Effects, Textures and Frames to your photos. They can be used individually, or in combination, to enhance your photos so that they will really stand out for your family and friends. To begin, open the image which you want to enhance with the Quick edit options:

The Effects panel has sub-categories for the main categories, i.e. the Seasons category has Summer, Autumn, Winter and Snow. Move the cursor over a category and click on the down-pointing arrow to view the sub-categories.

The Effects panel also has a Smart Looks option with five preset options for your photo. This is new in Elements 14.

Effects

To add photo effects to your images:

1 Click on the **Effects** button on the Quick edit toolbar

2 Click on one of the Effects options to apply that effect to the currently active image

Click on this button at the top of the Effects panel to reset the image to its original state, regardless of how many different options have been selected from the Effects panel.

...cont'd

Textures

To add texture effects to your images:

1 Click on the **Textures** button on the Quick edit editing panel

2 Click on one of the Textures options to apply that to the currently active image

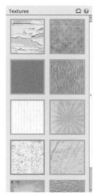

Textures are applied as an effect on the currently open image; they cover the image as a separate layer.

Frames

To add frame effects to your images:

1 Click on the **Frames** button on the Quick edit toolbar

2 Click on one of the Frames options to apply that to the currently active image

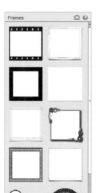

The effects are added to the image:

Save the file in a .PSD or .PDD format (a proprietary Photoshop format) to preserve the items added in Quick edit mode, so that they can be edited again when the file is opened. Save it in a .JPEG format to merge all of the layers, in which case they will not be able to be edited separately.

Use the options on these two pages for creative effects, particularly if you want to create items such as photo cards.

Using Guided Edit Mode

In Elements, the Guided edit function has been enhanced to make it easier to perform both simple editing functions, and also more complex image-editing processes that consist of a number of steps. To use the various functions of Guided edit mode:

1 Open an image and click on the **Guided** button

2 Click on the buttons at the top of the Guided edits window to view the different categories

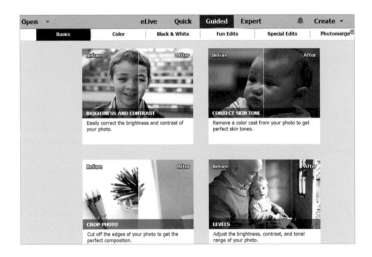

3 Items in each category have a thumbnail image that shows the **Before** and **After** effects for each item. Drag the slider across the thumbnail to view the effect for a greater or lesser amount of the thumbnail

Applying Guided edits

The process for Guided edits is the same regardless of the type of edit that has been selected:

1 Apply the Guided edit effect that has been selected. Different categories have varying numbers of steps; the **Basics** category has the fewest number of steps

For details of some of the Guided edits effects see pages 92-102.

2 Click on the **Next** button once the Guided edits have been completed, to save the final image

Next

If you do not like an effect that has been applied, click on the **Cancel** button.

3 Specify how you want to save and/or share the final image

Click on the **Save** button to save the final image with the same final name, and in the same file format. Click on the **Save As** button to save it as a new image with either a new file name or in a new file format, or both.

4 Click on the **Done** button

Done

Photomerge Effects

Within Elements, there are a number of Photomerge effects that can be used to combine elements from different photos to create a new image. This can be used to remove items from photos, combine elements from two or more photos, and match the exposure from different photos.

To access the Photomerge options, select **Guided > Photomerge** from within any of the Editor modes.

The Photomerge options are:

- **Compose**. This can be used to merge a part of one image with the background of another. This is a good option if you want to include people from one photo and transfer them into another photo.

- **Exposure**. This can be used to create a well-exposed photo from a series of photos of the same shot, that have different exposures, i.e. one may be over-exposed and another under-exposed. The Photomerge effect combines the photos so that the final one is correctly exposed. This can be done with the **Automatic** option, or the **Manual** one.

- **Faces**. This is an option for combining features of two faces together. This is done by opening photos of two people and then aligning the features of one so that they are merged with the other. The is a fun effect that can be used to combine faces of family members or two friends.

- **Group Shot**. This can be used to add or delete people from group shots. This is done by opening two or more, photos of the group. Use the **Pencil** tool to merge a person from one photo into the other and the **Eraser** tool to delete any areas that you do not want copied to the new photo.

- **Scene Cleaner**. This can be used to remove unwanted elements in a photo. This is done by using two or more similar photos, with elements that you want to remove, then merging the elements that you want to keep into the final photo. This is a good option if a single object has spoilt what is otherwise a good photo.

- **Panorama**. This can be used to create panoramas with two or more photos (see pages 89-90 for details).

For the Exposure Photomerge function, all of the photos used have to be of exactly the same shot, otherwise there will be some overlap in the final image.

The Pencil tool is used for several of the Photomerge options. It is used to draw over an area in a source image that is then merged into the final image.

Creating Panoramas

For anyone who takes landscape pictures, sooner or later the desire to create a panorama occurs. With film-based cameras, this usually involves sticking several photographs together to create the panorama, albeit a rather patchwork one. With digital images, the end result can look a lot more professional, and Elements has a dedicated function for achieving this: the Photomerge Panorama.

When creating a panorama there are a few rules to follow:

- If possible, use a tripod to ensure that your camera stays at the same level for all of the shots.

- Keep the same exposure settings for all images.

- Make sure that there is a reasonable overlap between images (about 20%). Some cameras enable you to align the correct overlap between the images.

- Keep the same distance between yourself and the object you are capturing, otherwise the end result will look out of perspective.

To create a panorama:

1 In Expert edit mode, open two or more images and select **Guided > Photomerge > Photomerge Panorama** from the Menu bar

2 Click on the **Auto Panorama** button to create the panorama automatically from the selected images

Auto Panorama

Auto select the Panorama layout based on my Images.

3 Click on the **Create Panorama** button

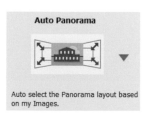

Create Panorama

Beware

Do not include too many images in a panorama, otherwise it could be too large for viewing or printing easily.

Hot tip

Panoramas do not just have to be of landscapes. They can also be used for items, such as a row of buildings or crowds at a sporting event.

Don't forget

In Step 2 there are other options for the style of the panorama.

Auto Panorama

Perspective

Cylindrical

...cont'd

4 The panorama will be created, but with gaps where the images could not be matched. The **Clean Edges** dialog box asks if you would like to fill in the edges of the panorama. Click on the **Yes** button to blend the empty areas with the background

5 Panoramas can usually be improved by applying color correction such as Brightness/Contrast and Shadows/Highlights. They can also be cropped to make a narrower panorama to highlight the main subject

5 Artistic Effects

This chapter shows how to create stunning effects and features, to give your photos the "wow" factor.

Zoom Burst

The Zoom Burst effect is a very dramatic one that can create a sense of motion and vibrancy in a photo. To use this effect:

Hot tip

It is most effective to use an image that has a sense of drama or motion.

Don't forget

Other **Fun Edits** include **Old Fashioned Photo**, **Pop Art**, **Puzzle Effect** and **Speed Effect**.

Don't forget

Within Guided edit mode, most of the options on the standard Menu bar are not available, as most of the editing functionality is done within Guided edit wizards.

1 In Editor, open the image to which you want to add the zoom burst effect

2 Access Guided edit mode. In the **Fun Edits** section, click on the **Zoom Burst Effect** button

3 Click on the **Crop Tool** button to crop the image so that the main subject is in the center, if required

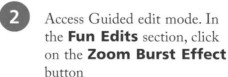

1. Use the Crop Tool to crop your image so that the primary subject is in the center.

Crop Tool

4 Click on the **Add Zoom Burst** button to apply the zoom burst effect to the photo

2. Click the Add Zoom Burst button to apply the effect to your image. Press multiple times to increase the effect.

Add Zoom Burst

5 Click on the **Add Focus Area** button and drag on the area of the image that you want to remain in focus. The rest of the image will retain the zoom burst effect

3. Click the Add Focus Area button and then click and drag on your image to specify the area of focus. Repeat as needed to increase the area of focus.

 Add Focus Area

Apply the Add Zoom Burst option more than once to make the effect more dramatic, but be careful not to overdo it.

6 Click on the **Apply Vignette** button and apply a vignette effect which creates a dark, shadow border around the image

4. [Optional] Add Vignette to your image. Click the button again to intensify the effect.

Apply Vignette

7 Click on the **Next** button to access the options for saving the final image

Next

You can also crop a Zoom Burst image after it has been completed, as well as cropping it during the Guided edit.

Depth of Field

Depth of field is a photographic technique where part of a photo is deliberately blurred, for artistic effect. Traditionally, this has been done through camera settings, but in Elements the same effect can be created within the Guided edit mode. To do this:

1 Open the image to which you want to add the depth of field effect

94

2 Access Guided edit mode. In the **Special Edits** section, click on the **Depth of Field** button

3 Click on the **Simple** button

4 Click on the **Add Blur** button to add a blurred effect to the whole image

...cont'd

5 Click on the
Add Focus Area button

6 Drag on the image, covering the
area that you want to appear in focus

The most realistic depth of field effect is done by dragging the **Add Focus Area** tool from front to back, in a straight line. It can also be done diagonally, but this is not something that could easily be achieved with a camera.

7 Drag this slider to increase the amount of blur of the area
that is not in focus

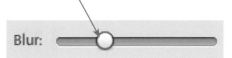

Add a reasonably large amount of blur to the image. This makes the depth of field effect more defined as a specific editing technique, rather than some of the image just appearing slightly out of focus.

8 Click on the **Next** button to access the options
for saving the final image

95

Out of Bounds

Out of Bounds can be used to display a section of an image without the rest of the original photo. This works best when there is one part of the image that obviously sticks out from the rest, such as part of a building, or someone's arm or leg. To do this:

1 Open an image that has an element that will naturally stick out from the rest

2 Access Guided edit mode. In the **Fun Edits** section, click on the **Out Of Bounds** button

3 Click on the **Add Frame** button

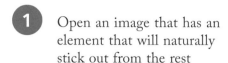

4 A default frame is added to the image. This can be sized by dragging the buttons situated around the border. It can be moved by clicking on the border and then dragging it into the required position. The area of the frame is the one that will form the main part of the final image

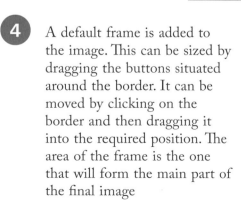

...cont'd

5 Hold down **Shift + Ctrl + Alt** (**Shift + Command key + Alt** on a Mac) to add perspective to the frame. This can be done by dragging the corner buttons and also those in the middle of each side

6 Click on the green check mark to apply the changes to the frame

7 The frame is displayed, with the rest of the image grayed-out

Don't forget

The frame contains the area that will be the main part of the image, not the Out of Bounds selection.

8 Click on the **Selection Tool** button

9 Drag over the area that will appear outside the main image

Beware

Be as accurate as possible when selecting the area in Step 9, so as to make the final effect as impressive as possible.

...cont'd

10 Click on the **Out of Bounds Effect** button

3. Out of Bounds Effect

11 The area selected in Step 9 now appears on its own, outside the area created by the frame

12 Click on the **Add Background Gradient** button to add a background gradient to the final image

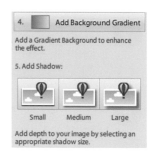

4. Add Background Gradient

Add a Gradient Background to enhance the effect.

5. Add Shadow:

Small   Medium   Large

Add depth to your image by selecting an appropriate shadow size.

13 Click on one of the **Add Shadow** buttons to add a drop shadow to the image

14 Click on the **Next** button to access the options for saving the final image

Next

Black and White Selection

A popular photo effect is to make part of an image black and white, leaving one element in color. To do this:

1 Open an image to which you want to apply the black and white effect

2 Access Guided edit mode. In the **Black & White** section, click on the **B&W Selection** button

3 Click on the **B&W Selection Brush** button and drag it over the area you want to select

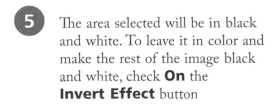

4 Click on the **Add** or **Subtract** buttons to add or remove areas of the selection

5 The area selected will be in black and white. To leave it in color and make the rest of the image black and white, check **On** the **Invert Effect** button

6 Click on the **Next** button to access the options for saving the final image

The selection brush in Step 3 is the Quick Selection brush, which selects areas of similar color as you drag it over the image.

Other **Black & White Guided edits** include **B&W Color Pop** (highlighting a single color in a photo), **High Key**, **Line Drawing** and **Low Key**.

To convert a photo to standard black and white, select **Enhance > Convert to Black and White** from the Menu bar in Expert or Quick edit mode.

Reflections

Reflections created within an image can be one of the most satisfying photographic effects. Images reflected in water, or on a clear surface, can create a very artistic and calming effect. However, it can be difficult to get the perfect reflection when taking an original photo. To help overcome this, Elements has a Guided edit option that can create the effect for you. To do this:

Beware

If you select an image that does not have enough detail in the foreground, the join with the reflected image may appear too severe and slightly unnatural.

1 Open the image you want to use for the reflection. If possible, use one with some objects in the foreground

Hot tip

Images with water in the foreground are a good option for reflection Fun Edits. However, use images that do not have too much water in the foreground as it will be doubled in the final reflection image.

2 Access Guided edit mode. In the **Fun Edits** section, click on the **Reflection** button

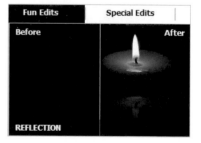

3 Click on the **Add Reflection** button

Add a reflection to your image by clicking the Add Reflection button.

4 The reflection effect is applied to the image

Experiment with different types of images and the reflection effect.

If a background color is used, this will be applied to the reflected image. However, this step does not have to be used.

5 Depending on the type of reflection you are creating, you can add a background color by selecting the **Eyedropper Tool** button and clicking on the **Fill Background** button

> 2. 🖊 Eyedropper tool
>
> Use the Eyedropper tool to choose a background color for your reflection.
>
> 3. 🖌 Fill Background
>
> Fill the background with your selected color.

6 Select the type of reflection effect you want to create

> 4. Apply an effect to make your reflection more realistic.
>
> Floor   Glass   Water

The Eyedropper tool in Step 5 can be used to select another color in the image, by simply clicking on it.

...cont'd

7 Each option has different dialog boxes which can be used to set the amount. Click on the **OK** button to apply the selected effect

8 The effect is applied to the reflected half of the image

9 Additional options can be applied to fine-tune the selected effect further

10 Click on the **Next** button to access the options for saving the final image

6 Beyond Basic Color Editing

This chapter looks at some of the more powerful features for image editing in Elements, so you can take your skills to the next level.

Hue and Saturation

The Hue/Saturation command can be used to edit the color elements of an image. However, it works slightly differently from other commands, such as those for the brightness and contrast. There are three areas that are covered by the Hue/Saturation command: color (hue), color strength (saturation) and lightness. To adjust the hue and saturation of an image:

1 Open an image

2 Select **Enhance > Adjust Color > Adjust Hue/ Saturation** from the Menu bar, in either Expert or Quick edit modes

3 Drag this slider to adjust the hue of the image, i.e. change the colors in the image

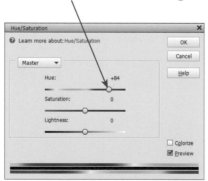

4 Drag this slider to adjust the saturation, i.e. the intensity of colors in the image

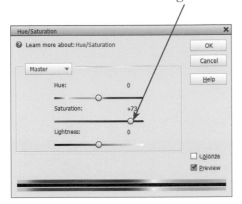

The Lightness option is similar to adjusting image brightness.

5 Check on the **Colorize** box to color the image with the hue of the currently-selected foreground color in the Color Picker, which is located at the bottom of the Toolbox

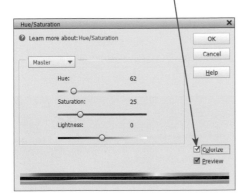

The Colorize option can be used to create some interesting "color wash" effects. Try altering the Hue slider once the Colorize box has been checked on.

6 Click on the **OK** button to apply any changes that have been made

OK

For more on working with color and the Color Picker, see pages 159-160.

105

Histogram

The Histogram in Elements is a device that displays the tonal range of the pixels in an image, and it can be used for very precise editing of an image. The Histogram (**Window > Histogram** in Expert edit mode) is a graph which displays how the pixels in an image are distributed across the image, from the darkest (black) to the lightest (white) points. Another way of considering the Histogram is that it displays the values of an image's highlights, midtones and shadows:

Hot tip

The keyboard shortcut for accessing the Histogram is F9.

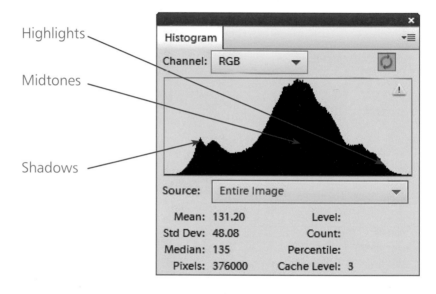

Highlights

Midtones

Shadows

Don't forget

The Histogram works by looking at the individual color channels of an image (Red, Green, Blue, also known as the RGB color model) or a combination of all three, which is displayed as the Luminosity in the Channel box. It can also look at all of the colors in an image.

Highlights

Midtones

Shadows

Don't forget

Image formats, such as JPEG, are edited in Elements using the RGB color model, i.e. red, green and blue, mixed together to create the colors in the image.

...cont'd

Ideally, the Histogram should show a reasonably consistent range of tonal distribution, indicating an image that has good contrast and detail:

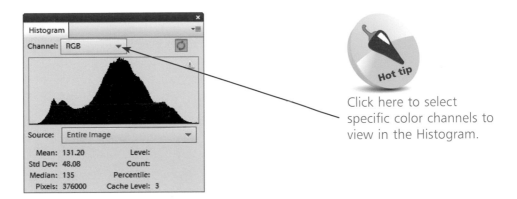

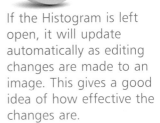

Click here to select specific color channels to view in the Histogram.

However, if the tonal range is bunched at one end of the graph, this indicates that the image is under-exposed or over-exposed:

Over-exposure

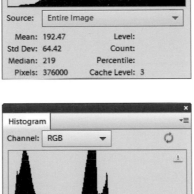

If the Histogram is left open, it will update automatically as editing changes are made to an image. This gives a good idea of how effective the changes are.

Under-exposure

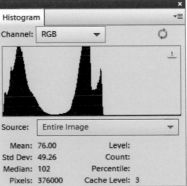

Levels

While the Histogram displays the tonal range of an image, the Levels function can be used to edit this range. Any changes made using the Levels function will then be visible in the Histogram. Levels allow you to redistribute pixels between the darkest and lightest points in an image, and also to set these points manually if you want to. To use the Levels function:

Hot tip

The Levels function can be used to adjust the tonal range of a specific area of an image, by first making a selection and then using the Levels dialog box. For more details on selecting areas see Chapter Seven.

Don't forget

In the Levels dialog box, the graph is the same as the one shown in the Histogram.

Don't forget

Image shadows, midtones and highlights can be altered by dragging the markers for the black, midtone and white input points.

1 Open an image

2 Select **Enhance > Adjust Lighting > Levels** from the Menu bar, in either Expert or Quick edit modes

Midtone input point

Black input point

White input point

Output points

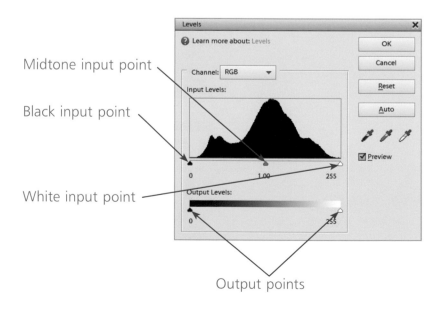

3 Drag the black point and the white point sliders to, or beyond, the first pixels denoted in the graph to increase the contrast

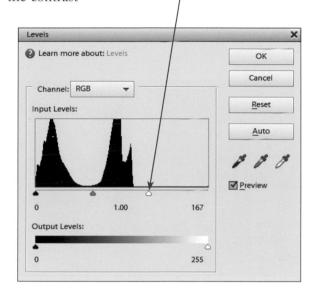

It is worth adjusting an image's black and white points before any other editing is performed.

Move the midtones point slider to darken or lighten the midtones in an image.

4 Drag the output sliders towards the middle to decrease the contrast

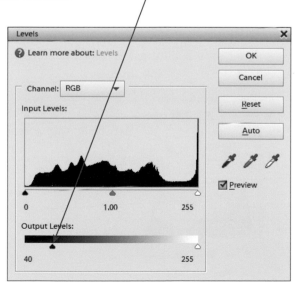

The Auto button, in the Levels dialog box, produces the same effect as using the **Enhance > Auto Levels** command from the Menu bar.

Adjustments with Levels

Although there is an Auto Levels function within Elements, more accurate editing can be done by using the Levels dialog box:

The Auto Levels option can be accessed by selecting **Enhance > Auto Levels** from the Menu bar.

The keyboard shortcut for accessing the Levels dialog window is Ctrl + L (Command key + L on a Mac).

By default, all of the color channels (RGB for Red, Green and Blue) are edited within Levels. However, click here to select the individual Red, Green and Blue channels so that they can be edited independently.

1 Open an image that is either too dark or too light (or requires the midtones to be edited)

2 Select **Enhance > Adjust Lighting > Levels** from the Menu bar

3 If there is no data at one end of the graph, it suggests an image is either too dark or too light (in this instance, too dark). Drag on this button to adjust the image

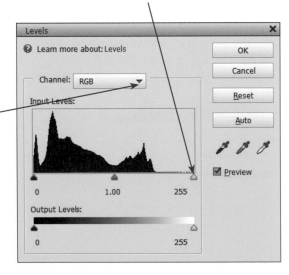

...cont'd

4 Drag the button to where the graph starts (or finishes). Ideally, the white and black buttons should be at the right and left of the graph

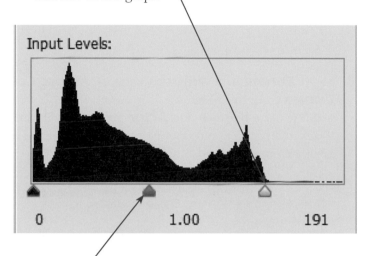

5 Drag on this button to adjust the midtones of an image, i.e. the color in the mid-range between white and black

6 The Levels editing effects are applied to the image

Hot tip

Adjusting the midtones manually is similar to using **Enhance > Adjust Lighting > Shadows/Highlights** from the Menu bar.

Don't forget

Levels can also be accessed and applied from Quick edit mode.

7 Click on the **OK** button to exit the Levels dialog window

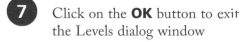
OK

Color Curves

If the colors are not ideal in a photo, one option for editing them is with Color Curves. This is done by editing the colors for different elements in the image, e.g. highlights, brightness, contrast and shadows. This can be done with preset options, or you can apply your own settings manually. To use Color Curves:

Don't forget

There is no keyboard shortcut for accessing the Color Curves dialog window.

1 Select **Enhance > Adjust Color > Adjust Color Curves** from the Menu bar. The Adjust Color Curves window has a **Before** and **After** preview panel at the top of the window, and options for automatic and manual adjustments at the bottom of the window

Don't forget

Color Curves edits the color using the overall color channels in an image. These are the individual Red, Green or Blue channels, or a combination of all three, the RGB channel.

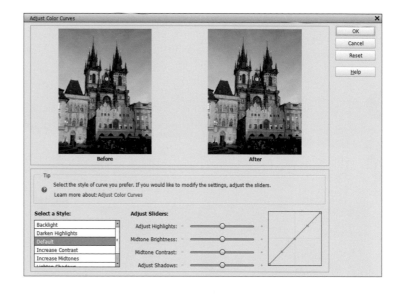

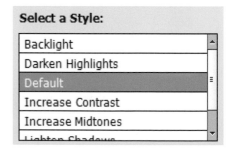

Hot tip

To avoid photos where the foreground subject is too dark, use the flash when taking a photo, even when there is bright sunlight behind the subject.

2 Under the **Select a Style** heading, select the area of color which you want to edit. These include **Backlight** (for images where the foreground subject is too dark), **Highlights**, **Default**, **Contrast**, **Midtones**, **Shadows** and **Solarize**

3 For each item selected in Step 2, the appropriate curve adjustments are made automatically (shown on the graph)

4 Drag the sliders under **Adjust Sliders** to edit the color elements in the image manually. As you drag the sliders, the graph moves accordingly

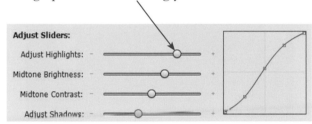

Dragging the sliders in Step 4 is a good way to see how the shape of the Color Curves graph affects the image.

5 The Color Curves editing effects are previewed at the top of the window

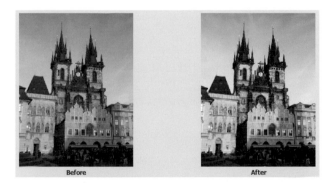

Exaggerated colors created with curves can make a striking photo, even if it is not completely realistic.

6 Click on the **OK** button to apply the changes, **Cancel** to remove them or **Reset** to return to the original image and continue editing it

Remove Color Cast

Even sophisticated digital cameras and smartphone cameras can sometimes misinterpret the lighting conditions of a scene, resulting in an unnatural color in the photo, known as color cast. To remove this:

Don't forget

There is no keyboard shortcut for accessing the Remove Color Cast dialog window.

Don't forget

Color cast is particularly common in indoor shots, taken without the flash, under artificial lighting. This is known as white balance, where the camera does not correctly interpret what white should be, and so all of the other colors in the photo are affected too. One way to overcome this is to change your camera's white balance settings if you are taking photos in artificial lighting.

Hot tip

Color cast can be edited manually within Levels. To do this, select one of the individual color channels (Red, Green or Blue) in the Levels dialog window and drag the input sliders accordingly.

1 In Expert or Quick edit modes, open the photo affected by color cast

2 Select **Enhance > Adjust Color > Remove Color Cast** from the Menu bar. Click on an area of the photo that should be black, white or gray. The overall color in the photo will be adjusted accordingly

7 Working with Selections

The true power of digital image editing comes into its own when you are able to select areas of an image and edit them independently.

This chapter looks at the various ways that selections can be made and edited, using the tools and functions within Elements.

About Selections

One of the most important aspects of image editing is the ability to select areas within an image. This can be used in a number of different ways:

- Selecting an object to apply an editing technique to it (such as changing the brightness or contrast) without affecting the rest of the image.

- Selecting a particular color in an image.

- Selecting an area on which to apply a special effect.

- Selecting an area to remove.

Expert edit mode has several tools that can be used to select items, and there are also a number of editing functions that can be applied to selections.

Two examples of how selections can be used are:

Once a selection has been made it stays selected, even when another tool is activated, to allow for further editing to take place.

If a selection is deleted, the space will be filled by the current background color in the Color Picker in the Toolbox.

1 Select an area within an image and delete it

2 Select an area in an image and add a color or special effect

The best way to deselect a selection is to click on it once with one of the selection tools, preferably the one used to make the selection. You can also choose **Select > Deselect** from the Menu bar.

Marquee Tools

There are two options for the Marquee tool: the Rectangular Marquee tool and the Elliptical Marquee tool. Both of these can be used to make symmetrical selections. To use the Marquee tools:

1 Select either the **Rectangular** or the **Elliptical Marquee** tool from the Toolbox. Select the required options from the Tool Options bar

To access additional tools from the Expert edit mode Toolbox, click on a tool and select any grouped tools in the Tool Options bar.

2 Make a symmetrical selection with one of the tools by clicking and dragging on an image

Elliptical selection   Rectangular selection

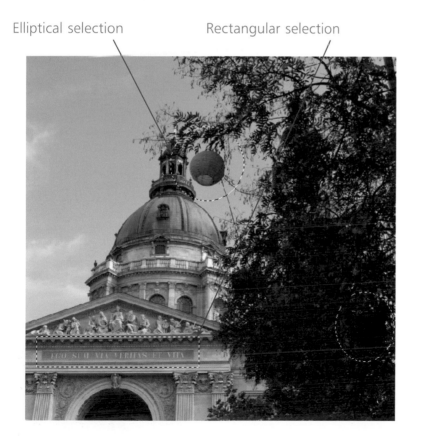

To make a selection that is exactly square or round, hold down **Shift** when dragging with the Rectangular Marquee tool or the Elliptical Marquee tool respectively.

Lasso Tools

There are three options for the Lasso tool, which can be used to make freehand selections. To use these:

Lasso tool

1 Select the **Lasso** tool from the Toolbox and select the required options from the Tool Options bar

2 Make a freehand selection by clicking and dragging around an object

Polygonal Lasso tool

1 Select the **Polygonal Lasso** tool from the Toolbox and select the required options from the Tool Options bar

2 Make a selection by clicking on specific points around an object, and then dragging to the next point

...cont'd

Magnetic Lasso tool

1 Select the **Magnetic Lasso** tool from the Toolbox and select the required options from the Tool Options bar

2 Click once on an image to create the first anchor point

3 Make a selection by dragging continuously around an object. The selection line snaps to the closest, strongest edge, i.e. the one with the most contrast. Fastening points are added as the selection is made

Hot tip

In the Tool Options bar for the Magnetic Lasso tool, the Contrast value determines the amount of contrast there has to be between colors for the selection line to snap to them. A high value detects lines with a high contrast, and vice versa.

Hot tip

The Frequency setting in the Tool Options bar determines how quickly the fastening points are inserted as a selection is being made. A high value places the fastening points more quickly than a low value.

Magic Wand Tool

The Magic Wand tool can be used to select areas of the same, or similar color. To do this:

In the Tool Options bar for the Magic Wand tool, the Tolerance box determines the range of colors that will be selected in relation to the color you click on. A low value will only select a very narrow range of colors in relation to the initially-selected one, while a high value will include a greater range. The values range from 0-255.

1 Select the **Magic Wand** tool from the Toolbox and select the required options from the Tool Options bar

2 Click on a color to select all of the adjacent pixels that are the same or similar color, depending on the options selected from the Tool Options bar

In the Tool Options bar for the Magic Wand tool, check on the **Contiguous** box to ensure that only adjacent colors are selected. To select the same, or similar, color throughout the image, whether adjacent or not, uncheck the Contiguous box.

Selection Brush Tool

The Selection Brush tool can be used to select areas by using a brush-like stroke. Unlike with the Marquee or Lasso tools, the area selected by the Selection Brush tool is the one directly below where the tool moves. To make a selection with the Selection Brush tool (this is also available in Quick edit mode):

1 Select the **Selection Brush** tool from the Toolbox and select the required options from the Tool Options bar

2 Click and drag to make a selection

3 The selection area is underneath the borders of the Selection Brush tool

The Selection Brush tool can be used to select an area, or to mask an area. This can be determined in the Selection drop-down box in the Tool Options bar.

The Selection Brush tool is best for selecting large areas that do not have to be too precise. For exact precision, use the Polygonal or Magnetic Lasso tools.

For all of the selection tools, hold down Shift to make another selection while retaining the original one.

Quick Selection Tool

The Quick Selection tool can be used to select areas of similar color by drawing over the general area, without having to make a specific selection. To do this:

Don't forget

The Quick Selection tool is also available from the Quick edit mode Toolbox.

1 Select the **Quick Selection** tool from the Toolbox

2 Select the required options from the Tool Options bar

Beware

If a very large brush size is used for the Quick Selection tool, e.g. 300 px (pixels) or above, you may select unwanted areas of the image by mistake.

3 Draw over an area, or part of an area, to select all of the similarly-colored pixels

Don't forget

As you drag the Quick Selection tool, it selects whichever areas of color over which is passes. As you drag over different areas of color, these will be selected too.

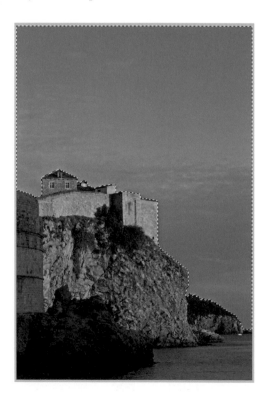

Smart Brush Tool

The Smart Brush tool can be used to quickly select large areas in an image (in a similar way to the Quick Selection tool) and then have effects applied automatically to the selected area. To do this:

1 Open the image to which you want to apply changes

2 Select the **Smart Brush** tool from the Toolbox

3 Select the editing effect you want to apply to the area selected by the Smart Brush tool, from the Tool Options bar

4 Select **Brush size** for the Smart Brush tool, from the Tool Options bar

5 Drag the Smart Brush tool over an area of the image. In the left-hand image below, the building has been selected and brightened; in the right-hand image the sky has been selected and enhanced

Don't forget

Multiple editing effects can be applied with the Smart Brush tool within the same image. This usually requires individually selecting different parts of the image and selecting the required effect.

Don't forget

Some of the other options for the Smart Brush tool include increasing the brightness or contrast, intensifying foliage in a photo, making lips redder and creating sepia images.

Inverting a Selection

This can be a useful option if you have edited a selection and then want to edit the rest of the image, without affecting the area you have just selected. To do this:

1 Make a selection

2 Choose **Select > Inverse** from the Menu bar

3 The selection becomes inverted, i.e. if a background object was selected the foreground is now selected

Feathering

Feathering is a technique that can be used to soften the edges of a selection by making them slightly blurry. This can be used if you are pasting a selection into another image, or if you want to soften the edges around a portrait of an individual. To do this:

1 Make a selection

2 Choose **Select > Feather** from the Menu bar

3 Enter a Feather value (the number of pixels around the radius of the selection

that will be blurred). Click on the **OK** button

4 Invert the selection, as shown on the previous page, and delete the background by pressing **Delete** on the keyboard. This will leave the selection around the subject with softened edges

The keyboard shortcut for accessing the Feather Selection dialog window is Alt + Ctrl + D (Alt + Command key + D on a Mac).

Feathering can also be selected from the Tool Options bar once a Marquee tool is selected, and before the selection has been made.

If required, crop the final image so that the feathered subject is more prominent.

Refining Selections

When making selections, it is sometimes difficult to exactly select the area that you want. In Elements 14 it is possible to refine the area of a selection, and also the edges around a selected item. To do this:

The **Refine Selection Brush** option can be used regardless of how the selection was made.

Click inside a selection to add to it; click outside it to subtract from it.

Click on the **View** box to select an option for the overlay that covers the current selection, so that you can see exactly what has been selected.

1 In Expert or Quick mode, make a selection with one of the selection tools

2 Select the **Refine Selection Brush** tool (grouped with the Quick Selection tool)

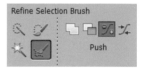

3 Click on this button to add or subtract from the selection with the cursor

4 Click on this button to smooth the edges of the selection by dragging the cursor over it

5 Select a size for the cursor for refining the selection, and the strength for how it snaps to neighboring pixels; the greater the strength, the more the selection will snap to pixels of similar color

6 Position the cursor inside or outside the selection. It appears as two circles, a smaller one inside a larger one. Use the circles to nudge the selection lines one way or another to refine the selection

Zoom in on a selection for the greatest accuracy in refining it.

Refining edges

It is also possible to add a range of refinements to the edges of a selection, which can be an excellent option for textures such as clothing or animal fur. To do this:

1 Once a selection has been made, click on the **Refine Edge** button in the Tool Options bar

Refine Edge...

There are some new adjustments in the Refine Edge option in Elements 14.

127

2 Select options here for how much of the edge is detected in terms of being refined. Select **Smart Radius** or enter a manual value for the radius

3 Select options here for how the edge is adjusted, using smoothing, feathering, contrast and moving the edge. Click **OK**

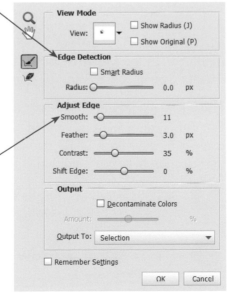

The Refine Edge options are particularly useful if you are copying a selection and pasting it into another image that has different textures.

Once an area has been moved and deselected, it cannot then be selected independently again, unless it has been copied and pasted onto a separate layer.

Don't forget

To deselect a selection, click once inside the selection area with the tool that was used to make the selection.

Hot tip

Selections can also be deselected by clicking on **Select > Deselect** from the Menu bar, or using Ctrl + D on the keyboard (Command key + D on a Mac).

Editing Selections

When you have made a selection, you can edit it in a number of ways:

Moving a selection
Make a selection and select the **Move** tool from the Toolbox. Drag the selection to move it to a new location.

Changing the selection area
Make a selection with a selection tool. With the same tool selected, click and drag within the selection area to move it over another part of the image.

Adding to a selection
Make a selection and click on this button in the Tool Options bar. Make another selection to create a single, larger selection. The two selections do not have to intersect.

Intersecting with a selection
To create a selection by intersecting two existing selections, make a selection and click on this button in the Tool Options bar. Make another selection that intersects the first. The intersected area will become the selection.

Expanding a selection
To expand a selection by a specific number of pixels, make a selection and choose **Select > Modify > Expand** from the Menu bar. In the **Expand Selection** dialog box, enter the amount by which you want the selection expanded.

Growing a selection
The Grow command can be used on a selection when it has been made with the Magic Wand tool, and some of the pixels within the selection have been omitted. To do this:

1 Make a selection with the **Magic Wand** tool and make the required choices from the Tool Options bar

2 Choose **Select > Grow** from the Menu bar

Depending on the choices in the Tool Options bar, the omitted pixels will be included in the selection.

8 Layers

Layers provide the means to add numerous elements to an image, and edit them independently from one another. This chapter looks at how to use layers to expand your creative possibilities.

Layering Images

Layering is a technique that enables you to add additional elements to an image, and place them on separate layers so that they can be edited and manipulated independently from other elements in the image. It is like creating an image using transparent sheets of film: each layer is independent of the others, but when they are combined, a composite image is created. This is an extremely versatile technique for working with digital images.

By using layers, several different elements can be combined to create a composite image:

Original image

Layers should usually be used when you are adding content to an image, as this gives more flexibility for working with the various image elements once they have been added.

Final image
With text, gradient and shapes added (four additional layers have been added).

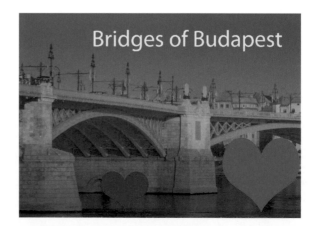

Text and shapes cannot be added together on the same layer.

Layers Panel

The use of layers within Elements is done within Expert edit mode and is governed by the Layers panel. When an image is first opened it is shown in the Layers panel as the Background layer. While this remains as the Background layer, it cannot be moved above any other layers. However, it can be converted into a normal layer, in which case it operates in the same way as any other layer. To convert a Background layer into a normal one:

1 Click on the **Layers** button on the Taskbar

2 The open image is shown in the Layers panel as the Background

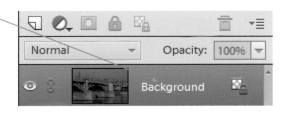

3 Double-click on the layer. Enter a name for it and click on the **OK** button

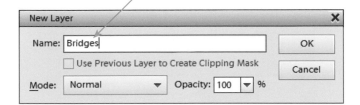

4 The Background layer is converted into a normal layer in the Layers panel

Adding Layers

New blank layers can be added whenever you want to include new content within an image. This could be part of another image that has been copied and pasted, a whole new image, some text or an object. To add a new layer:

1 Click here on the Layers panel

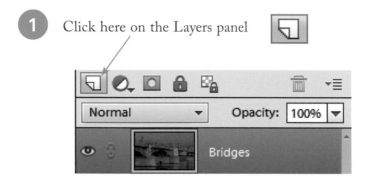

132

2 Double-click on the layer name and overtype to give the layer a new name

3 With the new layer selected in the Layers panel, add content to this layer. This will be visible over the layer, or layers, below it

Bridges of Budapest

Fill and Adjustment Layers

Fill and Adjustment layers can be added to images to give an effect behind or above the main subject. To do this:

1 Open the Layers panel and select a layer. The Fill or Adjustment layer will be placed directly above the selected layer

2 Click here at the bottom of the Layers panel

3 Select one of the Fill or Adjustment options. The Fill options are **Solid Color**, **Gradient** or **Pattern** Fill

Beware

For a Fill layer to be visible behind the main image, the image must have a transparent background. To achieve this, select the main subject. Choose **Select > Inverse** from the Menu bar and press the **Delete** key to delete the background. A checkerboard effect should be visible, which denotes that this part of the image is transparent. This only works on layers that have been converted into normal layers, rather than the Background one.

133

Don't forget

The Adjustments panel is also used for Levels, Brightness/Contrast, Hue/Saturation, Gradient Map, Photo Filter, Threshold and Posterize.

...cont'd

Hot tip

Fill and Adjustment layers can also be added from the Layer option on the Menu bar.

Hot tip

If you want to edit a Fill or Adjustment layer, double-click on its icon in the Layers panel and then apply the required changes.

Beware

If the opacity for a Fill layer is 100%, nothing will be visible beneath the layer.

4 For a Solid Color, Gradient or Pattern fill, the required fill is selected from the dialog box and this is added to the selected layer

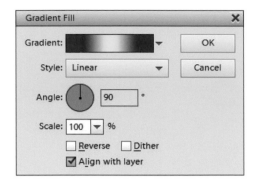

5 For an adjustment option, settings can be applied within the Adjustments panel

6 Once Fill and Adjustment settings have been applied, the effect can be edited by changing the opacity. This is done by dragging this slider

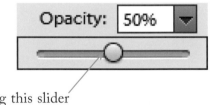

7 The opacity level determines how much of the image is visible through the Fill or Adjustment layer

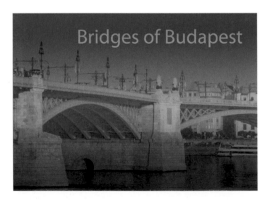

Working with Layers

Moving layers

The order in which layers are arranged in the Layers panel is known as the stacking order. It is possible to change a layer's position in the stacking order, which affects how it is viewed in the composite image. To do this:

1 Click and drag a layer within the Layers panel to change its stacking order

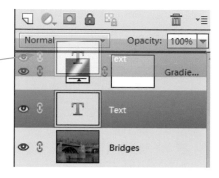

Layers cannot be moved underneath the Background layer, unless it has been renamed.

Hiding layers

Layers can be hidden while you are working on other parts of an image. However, the layer is still part of the composite image – it has not been removed. To hide a layer:

1 Click here so that a line appears through the eye icon, and the layer becomes hidden. Click again to remove the line and reveal the layer

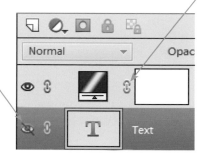

This icon indicates that the layer has a layer mask linked to it. This means that the mask will move with the layer, if it is moved. Click on the icon to unlink the layer mask from the layer (see page 136 for layer masks).

Locking layers

Layers can be locked, so that they cannot be edited accidentally while you are working on other parts of an image. To do this:

1 Select a layer and click here so that the padlock is activated. The padlock also appears on the layer itself

Layers can be deleted by selecting them and clicking on the **Trash** icon in the Layers panel. However, this also deletes all of the content on that layer.

Layer Masks

Because layers can be separated within an individual image, there is a certain amount of versatility in terms of how different layers can interact with each other. One of these ways is to create a layer mask. This is a top-level layer, through which an area is removed so that the layer below is revealed. To do this:

1 Open an image. It will be displayed as the Background in the Layers panel. Double-click on this to select it

2 Give the layer a new name and click on the **OK** button

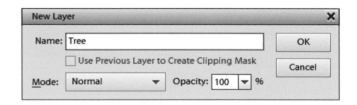

3 Click on the **Graphics** button on the Taskbar to access the Graphics panel

Graphics

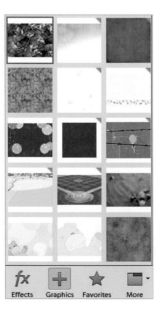

4 Select a graphic and double-click on it to add it as a layer to the current image. Initially, this is added below the open image. Rename the new layer

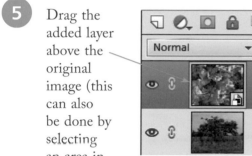

If a new layer is not renamed, it will automatically become the Background one.

5 Drag the added layer above the original image (this can also be done by selecting an area in another image, copying it and then pasting it above the existing image)

6 The graphic image layer now covers the original one

The top layer will obscure all layers below it, until either its opacity is reduced, or a layer mask is applied.

...cont'd

Don't forget

If the Brush tool is used to create the layer mask, this is done by drawing over the top layer of the image. As this is done, the layer below will be revealed. Change the level of Opacity in the Tool Options bar to change the amount that the layer below is shown through the top layer of the image.

Don't forget

The selected layer can also be deleted by pressing the **Delete** key on the keyboard.

Hot tip

Build up an image with several layer masks, to create an artistic effect.

7 Click here to apply a layer mask to the top layer

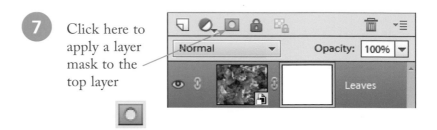

8 Select either one of the **Marquee** tools, the **Lasso** tools, or the **Brush** tool from the Toolbox

9 Select an area on the top layer and delete it, to display the image below it (**Edit > Delete** from the Menu bar)

10 In the Layers panel, the area that has been removed is displayed here

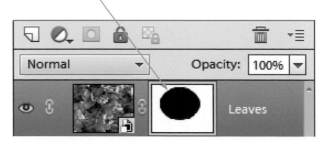

Opacity

The opacity of a layer can be set to determine how much of the layer below is visible through the selected layer. To do this:

1 Select a layer either in the Layers panel or by clicking on the relevant item within an image

2 Click here and drag the slider to achieve the required level of opacity. The greater the amount of opacity, the less transparent the selected layer becomes

3 The opacity setting determines how much of the background, or the layer below, is visible through the selected one and this can be used to create some interesting artistic effects, including a watermark effect if the opacity is applied to a single layer with nothing behind it

The background behind an image, to which opacity has been applied, can be changed within the Preferences section. Select **Edit > Preferences** from the Menu bar (**Adobe Photoshop Elements Editor > Preferences** on a Mac) and then select **Transparency** and edit the items in the Grid Colors box.

Different layers can have different levels of opacity applied to them.

Saving Layers

Once an image has been created using two or more layers, there are two ways in which the composite image can be saved: in a proprietary Photoshop format, in which case individual layers are maintained, or in a general file format, where all of the layers will be merged into a single one. The advantage of the former is that individual elements can still be edited within the image, independently of other items. In general, it is good practice to save layered images in both a Photoshop and a non-Photoshop format. To save layered images in a Photoshop format:

Hot tip

Before a layer is saved, it is possible to create a composite image consisting of a single layer. To do this, select **Layer > Flatten Image** from the Menu bar. To merge the existing layer and the one below it, select **Layer > Merge Down** from the Menu bar, and to merge all visible content (excluding any layers that have been hidden) select **Layer > Merge Visible**. If layers are flattened, they cannot then be edited independently.

Beware

Layered images that are saved in the Photoshop PSD/PDD format can increase dramatically in file size, compared with the original image or a layered image that has been flattened.

140

1 Select **File > Save As** from the Menu bar

2 Make sure Photoshop (*.PSD, *.PDD) is selected as the format

3 Make sure the Layers box is checked on

4 Click on the **Save** button

To save in a non-Photoshop format, select **File > Save As** from the Menu bar. Select the file format from the Format box (such as JPEG or TIFF) and click on the **Save** button. The Layers box will not be available.

9 Text and Drawing Tools

Elements offers a lot more than just the ability to edit digital images. It also has options for adding and formatting text, and creating a variety of graphical objects. This chapter looks at how to add and manipulate text, and also includes drawing objects.

Adding and Formatting Text

Text can be added to images in Elements and this can be used to create a wide range of items, such as cards, brochures and posters. To add text to an image:

1 Select the **Horizontal** or **Vertical Type** tool from the Toolbox

2 Drag on the image with the Type tool to create a text box

3 Make the required formatting selections from the Tool Options bar

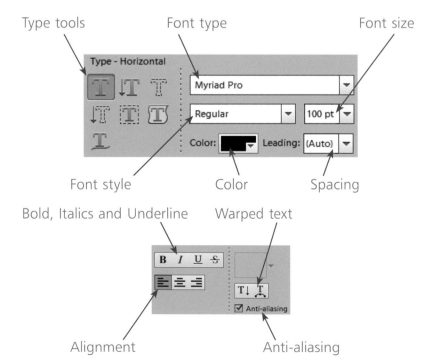

142

Type tools   Font type   Font size

Font style   Color   Spacing

Bold, Italics and Underline   Warped text

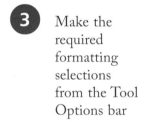

Alignment   Anti-aliasing

4 Type the
text onto
the image.
This is
automatically
placed onto
the image as
a new layer,
at the top of
the stacking order in the Layers panel

Each new text box is
placed on a new layer.

5 To move the
text, select
it with the
Move tool,
click and
drag it to a
new position

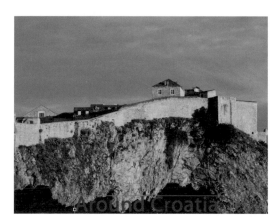

If there are two or more
text layers, they can be
moved above or below
each other in the Layers
panel.

To format text that has already been entered:

Hot tip

1 Select a **Type**
tool and drag it
over a piece of
text to select it

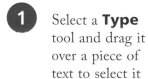

Individual words can
be selected by double-
clicking on them. Text
blocks, without a return,
can be selected by triple-
clicking on them. Text
blocks, with a return,
can be selected by
quadruple-clicking
on them.

2 Make the
changes in the
Tool Options
bar, as shown in Step 3 on the previous page

3 Click on the green check mark to
accept the text entry

Customizing Text

As well as adding standard text, it is also possible to add text to follow a selection, a shape or a custom path. This can be done within Expert edit and Quick edit modes.

Adding text to a selection
To add text to a selection within an image:

Don't forget

In Expert edit mode, select the Move tool and click and drag the text to move it with the selection area.

Hot tip

Text on Selection text should be reasonably large in size, so that it can be read clearly on the image.

1 Click on the **Type** tool and select the **Text on Selection** tool option

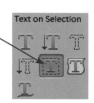

2 Drag over an area of an image to make a selection

3 Click on the green check mark to accept the selection

4 Click anywhere on the selection and add text. By default, this will be displayed along the outside of the selection

5 Format the text in the same way as with standard text

Adding text to a shape

To add text to a shape within an image:

1 Click on the **Type** tool and select the **Text on Shape** tool option

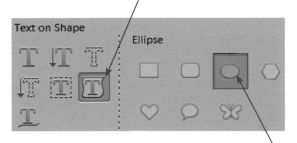

2 Click here in the Tool Options bar to select a shape

3 Drag over an area of an image to create a shape

4 Click anywhere on the shape and add text. Click on the green check mark as in Step 3 on the previous page

5 Format the text in the same way as with standard text

The butterfly shape is an artistic one, but it can be difficult reading text that is added in this way.

Once customized text has been added and accepted, it can still be edited in the same way as standard text, by using the Horizontal Type Tool and selecting the customized text.

Make sure that there is a good contrast between the text color and the background.

...cont'd

Adding text to a custom path

Text can also be added to a custom path that you draw onto an image. To do this:

The Modify button is used to edit an existing text path. See next page for more information.

1 Open the image onto which you want to create text on a custom path

If there are natural contours in an image, these can be used for the custom path.

2 Click on the **Type** tool and select the **Text on Custom Path** tool option. Make sure the **Draw** button is also selected

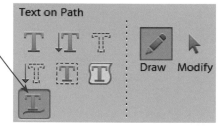

3 Draw a custom path on the image

More than one text path can be added to an image.

4 Click on the green check mark to accept the text path

5 Click anywhere on the custom path and add text

6 Format the text in the same way as with standard text

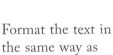

Myriad Pro | Color:
Regular | 48 pt

7 Click on the **Modify** tool in the Tool Options bar. This activates the markers along the custom path

8 Drag the markers to move the position of the custom path

9 The custom path can be used to position text in a variety of ways around objects or people

147

Distorting Text

In addition to producing standard text, it is also possible to create some dramatic effects by distorting text. To do this:

1 Enter plain text and select it by dragging a **Type** tool over it

2 Click the **Create Warped Text** button on the Tool Options bar

3 Click here and select one of the options in the Warp Text dialog box. Click on the **OK** button

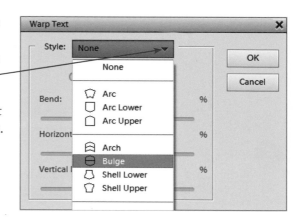

4 The selected effect is applied to the text

Text and Shape Masks

Text Masks can be used to reveal an area of an image showing through the text. This can be used to produce eye-catching headings and slogans. To do this:

1 Sclect the **Horizontal** or **Vertical Type Mask** tool from the Toolbox

2 Click on an image, then enter and format text as you would for normal text. A red mask is applied to the image when the mask text is entered

3 Press **Enter** or click the **Move** tool to border the mask text with dots

Text Mask effects work best if the text used is fairly large in size. In some cases it is a good idea to use bold text, as this is wider than standard text.

Text and shape masks are always red and do not show in the final image.

...cont'd

Text Masks can also be moved around in the original image, using the **Move** tool.

Once a Text Mask has been copied, it can also be pasted into other types of documents, such as Word and desktop publishing documents.

The Cookie Cutter shapes have several different categories which can be selected from the **Shapes** box above the current shapes. The categories include: Animals, Flowers, Music, Nature, Ornaments, Signs and Talk Bubbles.

4 Select **Edit > Copy** from the Menu bar

5 Select **File > New** from the Menu bar and create a new file

6 Select **Edit > Paste** from the Menu bar to paste the Text Mask into the new file

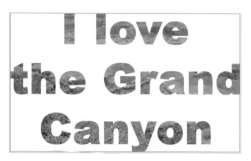

Cookie Cutter masks

A similar effect can be created with Shape Masks by using the Cookie Cutter tool (grouped with the Crop tool):

1 Select the **Cookie Cutter** tool in the Toolbox and click here to select a particular style in the Tool Options bar

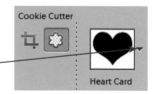

2 Drag on an image to create a cut-out effect

Adding Shapes

Another way to add extra style to your images is through the use of shapes. There are several types of symmetrical shapes that can be added to images, and also a range of custom ones. To add shapes to an image:

1 Click on the **Custom Shape** tool and select the type of shape you want to create

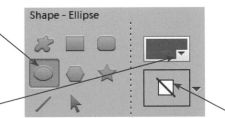

2 Select a color here

Click here to select a style for the shape. This includes **Bevels**, **Drop Shadows**, **Patterns** and **Glow** effects.

3 Click and drag on the image to create the selected shape

For the **Rectangle**, **Rounded Rectangle** and **Ellipse** shape tools, there is a box in the Tool Options bar to select whether the shape is **Unconstrained**, **Circle** (or **Square**), **Fixed Size** or **Proportional**. For Fixed Size you can specify a size; for Proportional you can set the height and width, and the shape will then always maintain these proportions.

4 If you want to change the color of the shape, click here in the Tool Options bar and select a new color. This can either be done before the shape is created or it can be used to edit the color of an existing shape, when selected with the **Move** tool

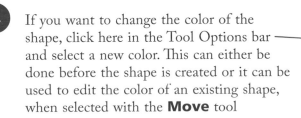

Paint Bucket Tool

The Paint Bucket tool can be used to add a solid color to a selection or an area in an image. To do this:

For more information on working with color, see pages 159-160.

The Paint Bucket tool can also be loaded with a pattern.

152

The higher the tolerance, the greater the area of color applied with the Paint Bucket tool.

Make a selection on an image and then apply the Paint Bucket tool to it, to get the color added exactly where you want.

1 Open the image to which you want to apply the solid color using the Paint Bucket tool

2 Select the **Paint Bucket** tool from the Toolbox

3 Select the **Opacity** and **Tolerance** in the Tool Options bar. The Tolerance determines how much of an image is affected by the Paint Bucket

4 Click once on an area of solid color with the Paint Bucket tool. The color in Step 2 will be applied

Gradient Tool

The Gradient tool can be used to add a gradient fill to a selection of an image, or an entire image. To do this:

1 Select an area in an image or select an object

If no selection is made for a gradient fill, the effect will be applied to the entire selected layer.

2 Select the **Gradient** tool from the Toolbox

3 Click here in the Tool Options bar to select pre-set gradient fills

Edit...

4 Click on a gradient style to apply it as the default

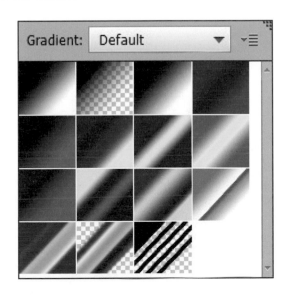

Gradient: Default

The default gradient effect in the Tool Options bar is created with the currently-selected foreground and background colors within the Toolbox.

...cont'd

5 Click here in the Tool Options bar to access the **Gradient Editor** dialog box

6 Click and drag the sliders to change the amount of a particular color in the gradient

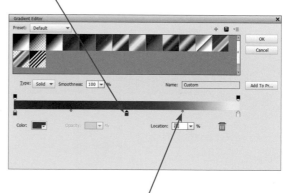

7 Click along here to add a new color marker. Click on the **OK** button

8 Click an icon in the Tool Options bar to select a gradient style

9 Click and drag within the original selection to specify the start and end points of the gradient effect

Brush and Pencil Tools

The Brush and Pencil tools work in a similar way and can be used to create lines of varying thickness and style. To do this:

1 Select the **Brush** tool or the **Pencil** tool from the Toolbox

2 Select the required options from the Tool Options bar

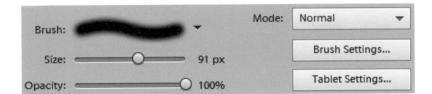

3 Click and drag to create lines on an image. (The lines are placed directly on the image. To add lines without altering the background image, add a new layer above the background and add the lines on this layer. They will then be visible over the background.)

155

The Mode options for the Brush and Pencil tools are similar to those for blending layers together. They include options such as Darken, Lighten, Soft Light and Difference. Each of these enables the line to blend with the image below it.

The Brush and Pencil tools are very similar in the way they function, except that the Brush tool has more options and can create more subtle effects.

Brush Tool Settings

The Brush tool is very versatile and there are numerous settings that can be applied, for different styles and effects. To use this:

156

1 Select the **Brush** tool from the Toolbox. The options show in the Tool Options bar

2 Click here to select a default brush style

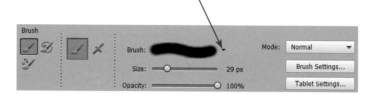

3 Select a brush size and style (Hard or Rounded edges) or scroll through the **Brush** box to select different brush styles

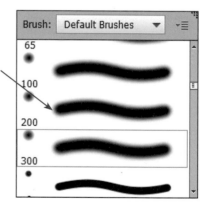

4 Click here to select a different brush type

...cont'd

5 Select a size and style for the brush selected in Step 4

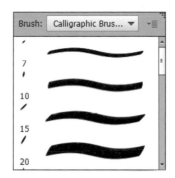

6 Click on the **Brush Settings** button in Step 2 to make selections for the appearance of the brush

7 Drag these sliders to apply the settings for each brush type

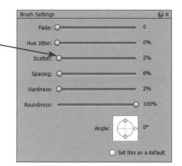

Here are some examples:

- From top to bottom, default brushes with hard edges, rounded edges and 50% opacity applied.

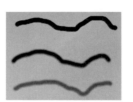

- From top to bottom, default brushes with **Scatter** applied at 50% and **Hue Jitter** at 50%.

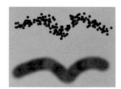

- From top to bottom, the **Calligraphic Brush** and the **Special Effects Brush (Drippy Watercolor)**.

Hot tip

Brush size can also be altered for custom brush styles created with the Define Brush command, see the first Hot tip on previous page.

Hot tip

Experiment with small changes initially in Step 7, to get an idea of what the effect looks like. Then build up the effect with a greater percentage, if required.

Beware

Do not use too many different brush styles on a single image as it could become a bit overpowering in terms of design.

Impressionist Brush Tool

The Impressionist Brush tool can be used to create a dappled effect over an image, similar to that of an impressionist painting. To do this:

1 Select the **Impressionist Brush** tool from the Toolbox

2 Select the required options from the Tool Options bar

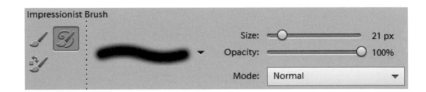

3 Click and drag over an image to create an impressionist effect

Working with Color

All of the text and drawing tools make extensive use of color. Elements provides a number of methods for selecting colors, and also for working with them.

Foreground and background colors

At the bottom of the Toolbox there are two colored squares. These represent the currently-selected foreground and background colors. The foreground color, which is the most frequently used, is the one that is applied to drawing objects, such as fills and lines, and also text. The background color is used for items such as gradient fills, and for areas that have been removed with the Eraser tool.

Foreground color   Swap foreground and background colors

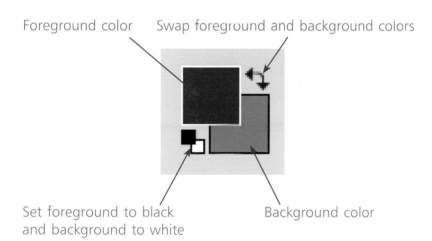

Set foreground to black and background to white   Background color

Color Picker

The Color Picker can be used to select a new color for the foreground or background color. To do this:

1 Click once on the foreground or the background color square, as required

Beware

Always check the foreground and background colors before you add any colors to an image, to ensure you have the right ones.

Hot tip

Whenever the foreground or background color squares are clicked on, the Eyedropper tool is automatically activated. This can be used to select a color from anywhere on your screen, instead of using the Color Picker.

Don't forget

Black and white are the default colors for the foreground and background colors, respectively.

...cont'd

If you are going to be using images on the web, check on the **Only Web Colors** box. This will display a different range of colors, which are known as web-safe colors. This means that they will appear the same on any type of web browser.

2 In the Color Picker, click to select a color

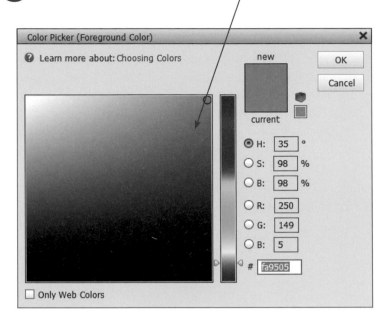

3 Click on the **OK** button

Color Swatches panel
The Color Swatches panel can be used to access different color panels that can then be used to select the foreground and background colors. To do this:

When the cursor is moved over a color in the Color Swatches panel, the tooltip displays a description of the color, e.g. RGB Green, or Pastel Red.

1 Select **Window > Color Swatches** from the Menu bar

2 Click here to access the available panels

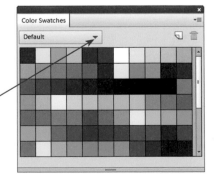

10 Becoming an Elements Expert

This chapter looks at some of the more advanced areas of Elements. These include working with the RAW file format, editing groups of images, creating and managing photo catalogs and resizing images.

Importing RAW Images

RAW images are those in which the digital data has not been processed in any way, or converted into any specific file format, by the camera when they were captured. These produce high quality images and are usually available on higher specification digital cameras. However, RAW is becoming more common in consumer digital cameras and they can be downloaded in Elements in the same way as any other image. Once the RAW images are accessed, the Camera Raw dialog box opens so that a variety of editing functions can be applied to the image. RAW images act as a digital negative and have to be saved into another format before they can be used in the conventional way. To edit RAW images:

Don't forget

The RAW format should be used if you want to make manual changes to an image to achieve the highest possible quality.

Beware

RAW images are much larger in file size than the same versions captured as JPEGs.

1 Open a RAW image in the Editor or from the Organizer

2 In the Camera Raw dialog box, editing functions that are usually performed when an image is captured can be made manually

3 Click here to adjust the White Balance in the image

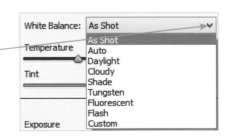

Hot tip

All images can be open in RAW by using the **File > Open in Camera Raw** command from the Menu bar.

4 Drag these sliders to adjust the Color Temperature and Tint in the image

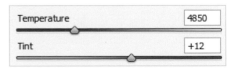

5 Drag these sliders to adjust the Exposure, Contrast, Highlights, Shadows, Whites and Blacks in the image

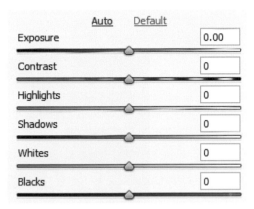

6 Click on the **Detail** tab and drag these sliders to adjust the Sharpness and Noise in the image

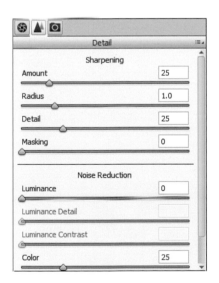

7 Click on the **Open Image** button. This opens the image in Expert edit mode, from where it can also be saved as a standard file format, such as JPEG

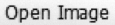

The Sharpness of an image refers to the contrast between adjoining pixels and can contribute to an image appearing more sharply in focus.

163

The Noise in an image refers to pixels that have not captured color accurately (mainly in low-level lighting) and can make images look 'speckled'. **Noise Reduction** in the RAW window can help reduce this, by dragging the available sliders.

Adding Filters

Filters are an excellent option for adding a range of effects to photos. They can be accessed and applied from the Menu bar in Expert or Quick edit mode (and also from the Filters section of the Effects panel). To add and modify filters:

1 In Expert or Quick edit mode, open the photo to which you want to apply a filter effect

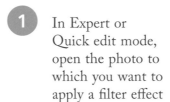

2 Select **Filter** from the Menu bar and select one of the filter categories and sub-categories

3 Some filter effects have a dialog box where additional settings can be applied

4 Some filters have preset options. Click on one to apply this automatically to the photo

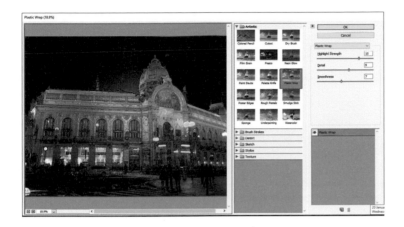

Don't forget

Each preset option overrides any previous ones that have been selected; they do not build up on top of each other.

5 Most filters have sliders that can be used to edit the effect that is being applied

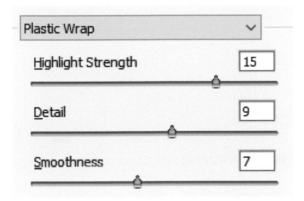

Hot tip

Use the Unsharp Mask filter to sharpen the focus of a photo. Although this is a filter, it is accessed from **Enhance > Unsharp Mask** on the Menu bar. In the **Amount** box, drag the slider to apply the amount of sharpening: a value of 100% or above is effective in most cases.

6 After you have made the desired changes, click on the **OK** button

7 The filter effect is applied to the photo

Editing Multiple Images

The rise of digital cameras and smartphones with photographic capabilities means that we are now taking more photos than ever. In terms of editing, this can result in a lot of work if you want to perform similar, or identical tasks on a number of images. However, in Elements there is an option for editing multiple files at the same time. This can be with a number of preset options, such as color quick fixes, renaming files and resizing files. To perform editing on multiple files:

Don't forget

The default file format for images taken with most digital cameras and smartphone cameras is JPEG (Joint Photographic Experts Group). However, this can be changed for a group of photos with the Process Multiple Files option.

1 In Expert edit mode, select **Edit > Process Multiple Files** from the Menu bar

2 The **Process Multiple Files** window contains all of the options for selecting and editing multiple files

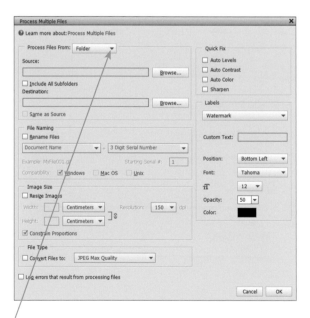

Hot tip

Use the **Opened Files** option in Step 3 to perform a task on specific files, rather than on a whole folder.

3 Click here to select options for the source location of the images to be edited. This can be either a folder, images imported from another location or the currently opened files

4 For the **Folder** option in Step 3, click on the **Browse** button, navigate to the required folder and click on the **OK** button

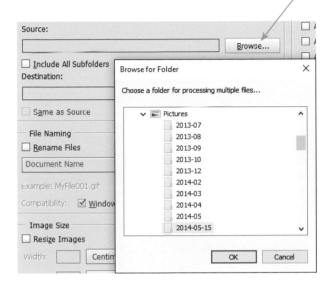

5 Select a destination folder in the same way as for selecting the source folder

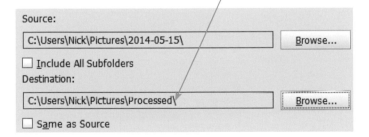

6 Under the **Quick Fix** section, check on any of the fixes that you want applied to all of the images. This is for **Auto Levels**, **Auto Contrast**, **Auto Color** and **Sharpen**

167

...cont'd

7 Under the **Image Size** section, check **On** the **Resize Images** checkbox and enter the required dimensions and resolution. If **Constrain Proportions** is checked **On**, only one of the Width or Height boxes has to be completed, as the other one will be adjusted automatically, in proportion

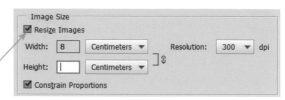

Beware

PDF and TIFF file formats generally produce larger files sizes than JPEGs, which is a file format specifically designed to compress file size.

8 Check **On** the **Convert Files to** button to select an option for converting the files into another file format, e.g. as PDFs or TIFFs

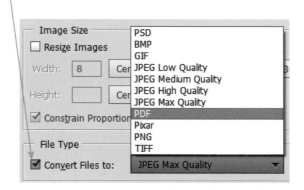

Don't forget

Once all of the required selections have been made for converting the files, click on the **OK** button.

OK

9 Check **On** the **Rename Files** button to rename the batch of files based on a base document name and a sequential identifier

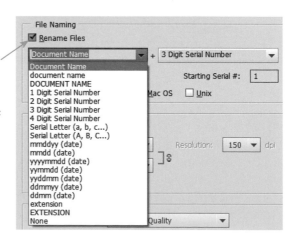

Applying Actions

Within Elements, there are a number of preset editing actions that can be applied to images repeatedly, without having to perform all of the separate tasks individually. To do this:

 1 In Expert edit mode, open the image to which you want to apply the action

2 Select **Window > Actions** from the Menu bar. Click here next to an Actions folder to expand it

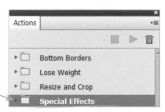

3 Click on an action to select it

4 Click on this button to perform the action

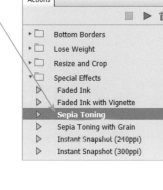

5 The action is performed and all of the required editing steps are applied to the image

The Actions panel does not have a keyboard shortcut.

You cannot create your own actions within Elements.

If you have the full version of Photoshop, you can import actions from here. To do this, click on the Actions panel's menu (top, right corner) and select **Load Actions**. Navigate to the Actions folder within the Photoshop program files (**Presets > Actions**) and select an action here. Click on the **Load** button to add it.

Managing Catalogs

Elements manages your photos in catalogs, in which all of your photos are organized. By default, this is done in a single catalog, known as My Catalog. This can contain all of your photos and you can search for them using keywords, tags or use albums. However, once you have thousands of photos, covering dozens of subjects, this can start to get a little overwhelming. One option is to create new catalogs that can be used for specific subjects, e.g. one for travel and one for business. To create and manage different catalogs:

Don't forget

Catalogs cannot be accessed from any of the Editor modes.

Don't forget

The existence of catalogs does not change the physical locations of photos; they still remain in their original folders.

Don't forget

When a catalog is selected in Step 2, there is also an option to Repair it. This can be done if images have been moved or deleted since the catalog was created.

1. In the Organizer, select **File > Manage Catalogs** from the Menu bar

2. The Catalog Manager dialog window displays the current catalog. Click on it here to select it and access options such as **Rename** or **Move**

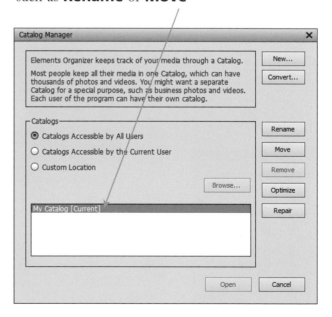

3. Click on the **New** button to create a new catalog

4 Enter a name for the new catalog

5 Click on the **OK** button

6 Click on the **Start Importing** button to add photos to the new catalog

7 Check **On** the **Pictures** checkbox in the left-hand panel and click on individual folders in the main window to select or deselect them

8 Click on the **Import** button to add selected folders

Make the names of catalogs as appropriate as possible to the intended subject matter.

Photos can be added to more than one catalog.

Blank catalogs can be created by clicking on the **Cancel** button in the **Import Media** window in Step 7. Media can then be added to the new catalog from a camera or memory card, or a folder, using the **Import** option.

171

...cont'd

9 The photos are imported into the new catalog

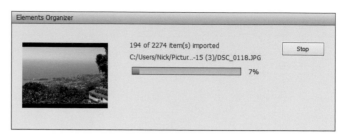

Hot tip

Click on the **Select All** or **Deselect All** buttons in Step 10 to select or deselect all of the keywords accordingly.

10 If keywords have been attached to any of the photos being imported, you will be able to include the keyword tags. Check **On** the checkboxes next to the required keywords and click on the **OK** button

11 Any photos that have been skipped for any reason, such as already being in the catalog, are detailed

Don't forget

If photos that are in an existing Elements catalog are imported into a new one, they will also remain in the original one.

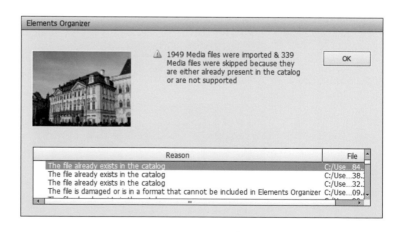

12 Click on the **OK** button   OK

...cont'd

13 The new catalog is created and displayed within the Catalog Manager dialog window

14 The photos in the new catalog are displayed in the same way as for the default catalog

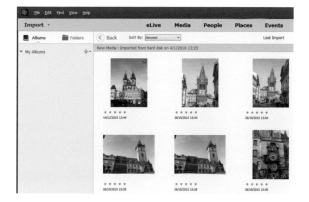

15 The name of the current catalog is displayed in the bottom right-hand corner of the Organizer window

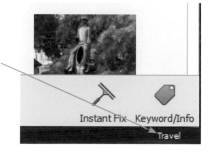

Don't forget

New catalogs can be edited by selecting them in the **Catalog Manager** window and clicking on the **Rename**, **Move**, **Optimize** or **Repair** buttons.

Beware

Catalogs can be deleted by selecting them and clicking on the **Remove** button. However, this can only be done when a catalog is not the one currently being viewed.

Hot tip

To change the catalog being viewed, select **File > Manage Catalogs** from the Organizer Menu bar. Select the required catalog in the **Catalog Manager** window and click on the **Open** button.

Viewing File Info

When digital images are taken, they create a considerable amount of related information, also known as metadata. To view this:

1 Open an image in Expert or Quick edit mode

2 Select **File > File Info** from the Menu bar

3 Click on the **Camera Data** button to view the information (metadata) that was created when the image was captured

> Camera Data

The **Shot Information** is created by the camera when a photo is taken.

174

4 The Camera Data information includes the **Camera Information**, i.e. the make and model of the camera and the **Shot Information**, i.e. Focal Length, Exposure, Image Size, Orientation, Resolution and Flash

Camera Information	
Make:	Canon
Model:	Canon EOS 350D DIGITAL; S/N: 2630703875
Owner:	
Lens:	

Shot Information	
Focal Length:	21.00 mm
Exposure:	1/30 sec; f/4.0; ISO 800; Aperture priority; Pattern metering
Image Size:	3456 x 2304
Orientation:	1 (Normal)
Resolution:	72.00 Pixel per Inch
Flash:	Did not fire

5 Click on the **Basic** button to add your own additional metadata to the image

> Basic

Add a **Copyright Status** and a **Copyright Notice** in Step 5 if your photos are going to be published in public, and you are concerned that they may be used by others without your permission.

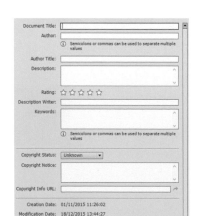

Save for Web

As digital cameras get more powerful in terms of the size of images that they can capture, one issue is how to use these images on the web or in email: the larger the image, the longer it takes to send in an email or upload on the web. To overcome this, there is an option to save an image specifically for web use. To do this:

1   Open an image in Expert or Quick edit mode

2   Select **File > Save for Web** from the Menu bar to open the Save for Web window

3   The size of the original image is shown in the left-hand panel; the new size in the right-hand panel

4   Click here to select a file format for the image for the web

5   Enter a new size for the image to reduce the physical size of it, e.g. from 3024 x 3024 pixels to 500 x 500 pixels

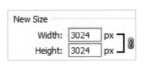

6   The size of the image in the right-hand panel is reduced accordingly (in this example to 208K)

The keyboard shortcut for the Save for Web dialog window is Alt + Shift + Ctrl + S (Alt + Shift + Command key + S on a Mac).

Next to the image size is an estimate for how long the image will take to download at different download speeds (which can be changed by clicking on the menu button next to the current speed).

Click on the **Save** button to exit the **Save for Web** window.

Image Size

The physical size of a digital image can sometimes be a confusing issue, as it is frequently dealt with under the term "resolution". Unfortunately, resolution can be applied to a number of areas of digital imaging: image resolution, monitor resolution, print size and print resolution.

Image resolution

The resolution of an image is determined by the number of pixels in it. This is counted as a vertical and a horizontal value, e.g. 4000 x 3000. When multiplied together it gives the overall resolution, i.e. 12,000,000 pixels in this case. This is frequently the headline figure quoted by camera manufacturers, e.g. 12 million pixels (or more commonly, 12 megapixels). To view the image resolution in Elements:

The keyboard shortcut for the Image Size dialog window is Alt + Ctrl + I (Alt + Command key + I on a Mac).

To view an image at its actual size, or the size at which it will currently be printed, select the **Zoom** tool from the Toolbox and select **1:1** or **Print Size** from the Tool Options bar.

1 Select **Image > Resize > Image Size** from the Menu bar

2 The image size is displayed here (in pixels)

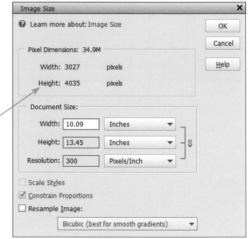

The Resolution figure under the Document Size heading is used to determine the size at which the image will be printed. If this is set to 96 pixels/inch, then the onscreen size and the printed size should be roughly the same.

Monitor resolution

Most modern computer monitors display digital images at between 72 and 96 pixels per inch (PPI). This means that every inch of the screen contains approximately this number of pixels. So, for an image being displayed at 100%, the onscreen size will be the number of pixels horizontally divided by 72 (or 96 depending on the monitor) and the same vertically. In the above example, this would mean the image, at actual size, could be viewed at 31 inches by 42 inches approximately (3027/96 and 4035/72) on a monitor. In modern web browsers, this is usually adjusted so that the whole image is accommodated on the viewable screen.

...cont'd

Document size (print resolution)

Pixels in an image are not a set size, which means that images can be printed in a variety of sizes, simply by contracting or expanding the available pixels. This is done by changing the resolution in the Document Size section of the Image Size dialog box. (When dealing with document size, think of this as the size of the printed document.) To set the size at which an image will be printed:

1 Select **Image > Resize > Image Size** from the Menu bar

2 Change the resolution here (or change the Width and Height of the document size). Make sure the Resample Image box is not checked (see page 178)

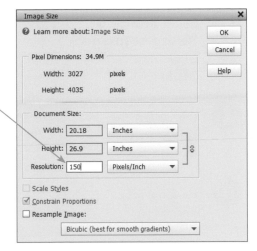

3 By changing one value, the other two are updated too

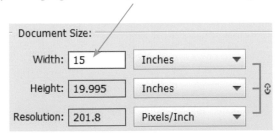

4 Click on the **OK** button

To work out the size at which an image will be printed, divide the pixel dimensions (height and width) by the resolution value under the Document Size heading.

The print resolution determines how many pixels are used in each inch of the printed image (PPI). However, the number of dots used to represent each pixel on the paper is determined by the printer resolution, measured in dots per inch (DPI). So if the print resolution is 72 PPI and the printer resolution is 2880 DPI, each pixel will be represented by 40 colored dots; i.e. 2880 divided by 72.

Resampling Images

All digital images can be increased or decreased in size. This involves adding or removing pixels from the image. Decreasing the size of an image is relatively straightforward and involves removing redundant pixels. However, increasing the size of an image involves adding pixels by digital guesswork. To do this, Elements looks at the existing pixels and works out the nearest match for the ones that are to be added. Increasing or decreasing the size of a digital image is known as "resampling".

Resampling

Resampling down decreases the size of the image and it is more effective than resampling up. To do this:

Don't forget

The process of adding pixels to an image to increase its size is known as "interpolation".

Hot tip

To keep the same resolution for an image, resample it by changing the Pixel Dimensions' height and width.
To keep the same Document Size (i.e. the size at which it will be printed) resample it by changing the resolution.

1 Select **Image > Resize > Image Size** from the Menu bar

2 Check **On** the **Resample Image** box

3 Resample the image by changing the pixel dimensions, the height and width or the resolution

4 Changing any of the values in the Image Size dialog box alters the physical size of the image. Click on the **OK** button

Beware

Make sure the Constrain Proportions box is checked on if you want the image to be increased or decreased in size proportionally.

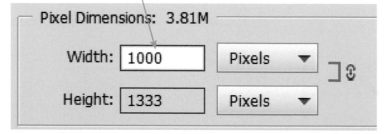

11 Printing Images

This chapter details sizing images and printing them in a variety of formats.

Print Size

Before you start printing images in Elements, it is important to ensure that they are going to be produced at the required size. Since the pixels within an image are not a set size, the printed dimensions of an image can be altered according to your needs. This is done by specifying how many pixels are used within each inch of the image. The more pixels per inch (PPI) then the higher the quality of the printed image, but the smaller in size it will be.

To set the print size of an image (in any of the Editor modes):

Don't forget

The higher the resolution in the Document Size section of the dialog, the greater the quality, but the smaller the size of the printed image.

1 Open an image and select **Image > Resize> Image Size** from the Menu bar

2 Uncheck the **Resample Image** box. This will ensure that the physical image size, i.e. the number of pixels in the image, remains unchanged when the resolution is changed

Hot tip

The output size for a printed image can be worked out by dividing the pixel dimensions (the width and height) by the resolution. So if the width is 2560, the height 1920 and the resolution 300 PPI, the printed image will be approximately 8 inches by 6 inches.

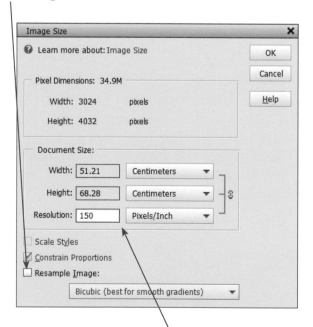

Image Size

Learn more about: Image Size

Pixel Dimensions: 34.9M

Width: 3024 pixels

Height: 4032 pixels

Document Size:

Width: 51.21 Centimeters

Height: 68.28 Centimeters

Resolution: 150 Pixels/Inch

☐ Scale Styles

☑ Constrain Proportions

☐ Resample Image:

Bicubic (best for smooth gradients)

OK

Cancel

Help

3 The current resolution and document size (print size) are displayed here

Don't forget

As long as the Resample box is unchecked, changing the output resolution has no effect on the actual number of pixels in an image.

4 Enter a new figure in the Resolution box (here, the resolution has been increased from 150 to 300). This affects the Document size, i.e. the size at which the image prints

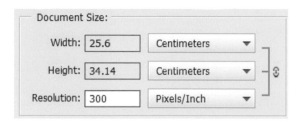

Viewing print size
In Expert mode, images can be viewed at their print size:

1 Click on the Zoom tool

2 In the Tool Options, click on the **Print Size** button

3 The image is displayed at the size at which it will be printed. Change the resolution to see how this changes the print size

Hot tip

The keyboard shortcut for accessing the Image Size dialog window is Alt + Ctrl + I (Alt + Command key + I on a Mac).

Don't forget

A resolution of 300 pixels per inch (PPI) is a good benchmark for printed images. However, a lower resolution will still produce a good quality and enable the image to be printed at a larger size.

Beware

The print size on screen may not be completely accurate, depending on the resolution of your monitor. However, it will still give a reasonably good idea of the size of the printed image.

Print Functions

The Print functions in Elements can be accessed from the Menu bar in either the Editor or the Organizer, by selecting **File > Print**. Also, all of the print functions can be selected from Create mode. To print to your local printer using this method:

The keyboard shortcut for printing images is Ctrl + P, in either Editor or Organizer mode (Command key + P on a Mac).

1 Select an image in either the Editor or the Organizer, click on the **Create** button and click on the **Photo Prints** button

The currently-active images are shown in the left-hand panel of the Print window.

2 Click on the **Local Printer** button

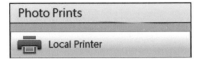

3 The main print window displays the default options for how the printed image will appear, and also options for changing the properties of the print

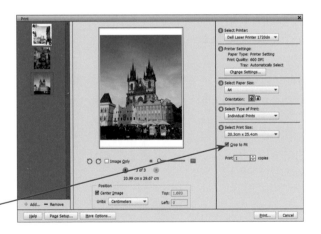

Check **On** the **Crop to Fit** checkbox to crop the photo to ensure it fits on the page. Check the photo to ensure that it still appears as required.

4 Click the **Add** button to include more images in the current print job, or select an image and click on the **Remove** button to exclude it

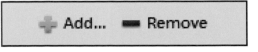

...cont'd

5 Use these options to rotate an image for printing, change its size, or position

Check on the **Center Image** box in Step 5 to have the image printed in the center of the page.

6 Click here to select a destination printer to which you want to send your print

7 Click on the **Change Settings** button to change the properties for your own local printer

8 Click here to select the paper size for printing

9 Click here to select the print type, i.e. the layout of the image you are printing

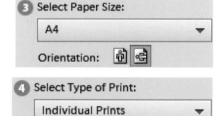

The other options for **Type of Print** in Step 9 are **Picture Package** and **Contact Sheet**. See next pages 184-185 for more details.

10 Click here to select the size at which you want your image to be printed

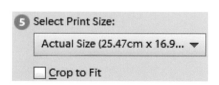

11 Click on the **Print** button to print your image with the settings selected above

183

Print Layouts

Rather than just offering the sole function of printing a single image on a sheet of paper, Elements has two options that can be used when printing images, which can help reduce the number of sheets of paper used.

Picture Package
This can be used to print out copies of different images on a single piece of paper. To do this:

When buying a printer, choose one that has borderless printing. This means that it can print to the very edge of the page. This is particularly useful for items such as files, produced as a Picture Package.

The Picture Package option is also available if you print photos using **File > Print** (or Ctrl + P, Command + P on a Mac) from the Menu bar. In the **Prints** dialog window, select **Picture Package** under the **Select Type of Print** heading.

The Picture Package function is useful for printing images in a combination of sizes, such as for family portraits.

1 Select an image in either the Editor or the Organizer, click on the Create button and click on the **Picture Package** button

2 The layout for the Picture Package is displayed in the main print window

3 Under **Select a Layout**, select how many images you want on a page and, if required, select a type of frame for the printed images

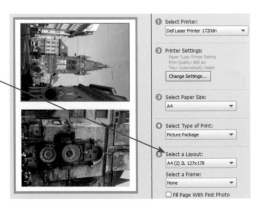

Contact Sheets

This can be used to create and print thumbnail versions of a large number of images. To do this:

1 Select an image in either the Editor or the Organizer, click on the Create button and click on the **Contact Sheet** button

2 The layout for the Contact Sheet is displayed in the main Print window

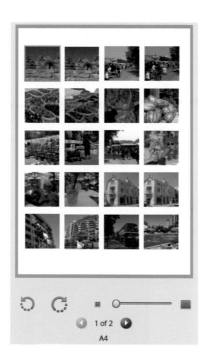

When a contact sheet is created, new thumbnail images are generated. The original images are unaffected.

Do not include too many thumbnails on a contact sheet, otherwise they may be too small to see any detail clearly.

3 Click under **Select Type of Print** and select the number of columns to be displayed on the contact sheet

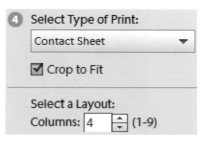

Creating PDF Files

PDF (Portable Document Format) is a file format that is used to maintain the original formatting and style of a document, so that it can be viewed on a variety of different devices and types of computers. In general, it is usually used for documents that contain text and images, such as information pamphlets, magazine features and chapters from books. However, image files, such as JPEGs, can also be converted into PDF and this can be done within Elements without the need for any other specialist software. To do this:

Don't forget

PDF files are an excellent way to share files so that other people can print them. All that is required is a copy of Adobe Acrobat Reader, which is bundled with most software packages on computers, or can be downloaded from the Adobe website at: www.adobe.com

1 Open an image and select **File > Save As** from the Menu bar

2 Select a destination folder and make sure the format is set to Photoshop PDF, then click **Save**

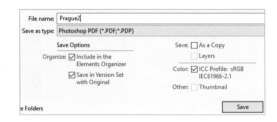

3 The PDF file is created and can be opened in Adobe Acrobat or Elements

Beware

PDF files are generally larger in terms of file size than standard image file formats such as JPEG.

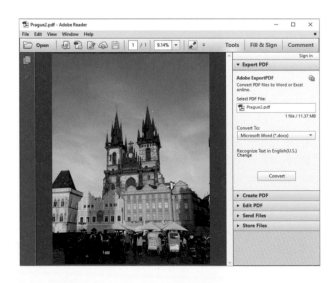

Index

189

Q

R

S

T